CW00550736

The Fragrant Scent

FREE COPY
NOT FOR SALE

THE PRINCE GHAZI TRUST FOR QUR'ĀNIC THOUGHT
and
THE ISLAMIC TEXTS SOCIETY

THE FRAGRANT SCENT:
On the Knowledge of Motivating Thoughts and Other Such Gems

ᶜAbd al-Raḥmān al-ᶜAydarūs

Translated by Mokrane Guezzou

The Prince Ghazi Trust
for Qur'anic Thought

Islamic Texts Society

This first edition published 2015 by

THE PRINCE GHAZI TRUST FOR QUR'ANIC THOUGHT

&

THE ISLAMIC TEXTS SOCIETY

MILLER'S HOUSE

KINGS MILL LANE

GREAT SHELFORD

CAMBRIDGE CB22 5EN, UK.

British Library Cataloguing-in-Publication Data.
A catalogue record for this book is
available from the British Library.

ISBN: 978 1903682 92 0 cloth
ISBN: 978 1903682 93 7 paper

Printed in Turkey by Mega Printing

CONTENTS

THE FRAGRANT SCENT

FOREWORD

In the Name of God, the Compassionate, the Merciful

Praise be to God. The Prince Ghazi Trust for Qur'anic Thought is very gratified—together with the Islamic Texts Society and the translator Mr Mokrane Guezzou—to make available for the first time in English, *The Fragrant Scent: On the Knowledge of Motivating Thoughts and Other Such Gems* by Abu'l-Marāḥim ʿAbd al-Raḥmān b. Muṣṭafā b. Shaykh al-ʿAydarus (1135–1192 AH/1722–1778 CE).

The reason the Prince Ghazi Trust for Qur'anic Thought has sponsored this translation is not because it is a work of Islamic mysticism, but rather because it is a Qur'an-based work of spiritual psychology. Indeed, it would be difficult to find, in the whole of Islamic history and religious literature, so short a work that illustrates so perfectly the Qur'anic basis for operative spiritual psychology. As such, this work truly shows the Qur'an as both the theoretic and practical basis of psychology in Islam. Psychology can then be understood—alongside doctrine, theology, sacred law, spiritual practice, ethics, Arabic linguistic sciences, hermeneutics, anthropology, sociology, history, philosophy, epistemology, cosmology, metaphysics, numerology, and even zoology, oneirology and other subjects—as an integral topic and part of Qur'anic thought. God says, *There is no animal on the earth and no bird that flies with its wings, but they are communities like to you. We have neglected nothing in the Book; then to their Lord they shall be gathered.* (*Al-Anʿām,* VI.38)

We hope that the translation of this work will prove of interest and benefit. We beg of readers their prayers for all involved starting of course with author himself. And may peace and blessings be upon the Prophet Muḥammad.

Ghazi bin Muhammad bin Talal
1436 AH/2015 CE

EDITOR'S INTRODUCTION

The Fragrant Scent: On the Knowledge of Motivating Thoughts and Other Such Gems by the great eighteenth-century Yemenī scholar, ʿAbd al-Raḥmān b. Muṣṭafā al-ʿAydarūs (1135–1192/1723–1778), is considered by many to be the best single work on the subject of motivating thoughts (*khāṭir*, pl. *khawāṭir*). *The Fragrant Scent* takes the form of a short commentary written by ʿAydarūs on one of his own didactic poems about *khawāṭir*, and was inspired by Abū Ḥafṣ al-Suhrawardī's famous Sufi manual, *The Gifts of Knowledge* (ʿAwārif al-maʿārif). The work is addressed to the spiritual wayfarer (*sālik*) and offers sound guidance about how to progress along the path to God without stumbling or slipping into heresy.

ʿAbd al-Raḥmān b. Muṣṭafā al-ʿAydarūs

Sayyid Abū al-Marāḥim ʿAbd al-Raḥmān b. Muṣṭafā b. Shaykh al-ʿAydarūs was descended from the Saqqāf branch of the illustrious family of the Bā ʿAlawī *sayyids* of Hadramawt and was their most prolific writer.[1] He was descended from the Prophet Muḥammad through ʿAlī and Ḥusayn, and his ancestors included the revered Abū Bakr b. ʿAbd Allāh al-ʿAydarūs of Aden (d. 914/1508).[2] By the stand-

1 See the biographical entries about him in Muḥammad Khalīl b. ʿAlī al-Murādī, *Silk al-durar fī aʿyān al-qarn al-thānī ʿashar*, Beirut: Dār al-Bashā'ir/Dār Ibn Ḥazm, 1988, vol. II, p. 328; ʿAbd al-Raḥmān b. Ḥasan al-Jabartī, *ʿAjā'ib al-āthār fī al-tarājim wa'l-akhbār aw Ta'rīkh al-Jabartī*, Cairo: al-Maṭbaʿa al-ʿĀmiriyya al-Sharafiyya, 1322/1904, vol. II, pp. 28–35; ʿAbd al-Ḥayy b. ʿAbd al-Kabīr al-Kattānī, *Fihris al-fahāris wa'l-athbāt wa-muʿjam al-maʿājim wa'l-mashyakhāt wa'l-musalsalāt*, ed. Iḥsān ʿAbbās, Beirut: Dār al-Gharb al-Islāmī, [no date]; Khayr al-Dīn al-Ziriklī, *al-Aʿlām: Qāmūs tarājim li-ashhar al-rijāl wa'l-nisā' min al-ʿarab wa'l-mustaʿribīn wa'l-mustashriqīn*, Beirut: Dār al-ʿIlm li'l-Malāyīn, 1984, vol. III, p. 338; and ʿUmar Riḍā al-Kaḥḥāla, *Muʿjam al-mu'allifīn: Tarājim muṣannifī al-kutub al-ʿarabiyya*, Beirut: Dār Iḥyā' al-Turāth al-ʿArabī, [no date], vol. V, p. 195.

2 On the history of the ʿAydarūs family, see Esther Peskes, *al-Aidarus und seine Erben*, Stuttgart: Franz Steiner Verlag, 2005.

ards of the time, ʿAydarūs was very well-travelled and so had many opportunities to expand his knowledge of the traditional sciences.

ʿAbd al-Raḥmān al-ʿAydarūs was born in Tarim in 1135/1723 and studied the religious sciences with the city's eminent scholars during his early years, including with his grandfather, Shaykh b. Muṣṭafā al-ʿAydarūs, his father, Muṣṭafā, and Shaykh ʿAbd al-Raḥmān b. ʿAbd al-Allāh Bilfaqīh. In his late teens, ʿAydarūs made his way to Gujarat in India to continue his studies, and after travelling as far as Java, he returned to Hadramawt. His travels continued when he embarked upon the pilgrimage; once in the Hijaz, he spent several years living in Ṭā'if before making his way to Egypt in 1174/1760. He made several visits to Cairo in the latter part of his life and died there in 1192/1778.

In each place that he visited, ʿAydarūs sought out the leading scholars of the day to further his learning and spiritual understanding; in time, he came to be a renowned scholar with disciples of his own. His wisdom and erudition attracted the attention of many students, the most notable of whom were: his son, ʿAbd al-Raḥmān; the distinguished Yemenī scholar, Muḥammad Murtaḍā al-Zabīdī; the historian, ʿAbd al-Raḥmān al-Jabartī, and his companion, Muḥammad al-Tāwadī, a Maghribī scholar of astronomy and mathematics; the Egyptian scholar, Sulaymān al-Jamal; and, the Yemenī *Ḥadīth* scholar, ʿAbd al-Raḥmān b. Sulaymān al-Ahdal.

As a member of the Bā ʿAlawī, ʿAydarūs was also an adherent of the ʿAlawiyya Sufi Order (*ṭarīqa*), which was founded by Muḥammad b. ʿAlī, known as al-Faqīh al-Muqaddam (d. 653/1255). A distinctive feature of the ʿAlawiyya *ṭarīqa* was the importance placed on both spirituality and genealogy. This was formally expressed by a dual chain of spiritual descent (*silsila*) that represented both the familial bonds that connected its adherents back to the Prophet himself, and those bestowed through initiation into the order.[1]

1 For an in-depth discussion of this subject, see Anne Bang, *Sufis and Scholars of the Sea: Family Networks in East Africa, 1860–1925*, London: Routledge, 2003, pp. 13–15. The *ṭarīqa*'s dual *silsila* is presented on p. 14, fig. 1.1.

The first, genealogical *silsila* extended back to the Prophet through the family lineage via the founder of the Bā ʿAlawī, Aḥmad b. ʿĪsā al-Muhājir, who emigrated to Hadramawt from Basra in the fourth/tenth century. This *silsila* was proof of the *baraka* with which descendants of the Prophet are believed to be particularly endowed. Consequently, a distinguishing feature of the literature produced by the order's adherents (including the works of ʿAydarūs, author of *The Fragrant Scent*) was the attention paid to the family's noble forefathers. This took the form of recording their biographies, recounting tales of their spiritual exploits and documenting the location of their graves.[1] These forefathers were held up as exemplars for the community; by emulating them, the spiritual seeker could hope to embody the conduct of the Prophet himself. It is therefore unsurprising that, despite the diverse origins of ʿAydarūs's teachers over the years and his indebtedness to scholarship from beyond Yemen, a large proportion of the Sufi authorities referred to in *The Fragrant Scent* were Bā ʿAlawīs.

The second *silsila* of the ʿAlawiyya *ṭarīqa* was spiritual, and was linked by master-disciple relationships extending back through al-Faqīh al-Muqaddam to the famous saint Abū Madyan (progenitor of the Shādhilī *ṭarīqa*), whose spiritul lineage included many illustrious Sufis, among them Ghazālī, Juwaynī, Abū Ṭālib al-Makkī, Junayd, Sarī Saqaṭī and Maʿrūf Kharkhī. In turn, the regard with which these Sufis (and those of the Shādhiliyya) were held is evident in ʿAlawī writings on Sufism—including *The Fragrant Scent*. ʿAydarūs referred to many of them in the present work and made particular reference to the works of Ghazālī, Abū Ḥafṣ al-Suhrawardī and Ibn ʿAṭā' Allāh al-Iskandarī.

In addition to *The Fragrant Scent*, ʿAydarūs wrote more than 60 other works over the course of his lifetime, ranging from commen-

1 As an example of this literary tradition, see ʿAydarūs b. ʿUmar b. ʿAydarūs al-Ḥabshī, *ʿIqd al-yawāqīt al-jawhariyya wa-simṭ al-ʿayn al-dhahabiyya bi-dhikr ṭarīq al-sādāt al-ʿalawiyya*, Cairo: al-Maṭbaʿa al-ʿĀmiriyya al-Sharafiyya, 1317/1899.

taries and *Ḥadīth* works, to mystical love poems and hagiographies of members of the ʿAydarūs family.[1] Regrettably, only a small number of his works have been published and little is known about him in the English-speaking world. This translation of *The Fragrant Scent* is therefore a significant step in filling this gap and makes it an important contribution to the study of Sufism in Yemen.

The Fragrant Scent

The Fragrant Scent: On the Knowledge of Motivating Thoughts and Other Such Gems (al-ʿArf al-ʿāṭir fī maʿrifat al-khawāṭir wa-ghayrihā min al-jawāhir) is a work that comprehensively explores one particular aspect of the Sufi path to God: the dangers and benefits that come from motivating thoughts. *Khawāṭir* were an important topic in premodern Islamic thought and the literature on the subject is extensive.[2] *Khawāṭir* are fleeting or passing thoughts and impulses (translated in the present work as 'motivating thoughts'), and ʿAydarūs described their three distinguishing characteristics as follows. Firstly, he wrote that 'a motivating thought is the beginning of an action and its initiation;' in other words, the motivating thought brings ideas to the attention of an individual and initiates a reaction or a response to those ideas. Secondly, the *khawāṭir* are 'an inner mode of expression' that come upon the heart (*qalb*) alone—not the spirit, ego or breast. And thirdly, there are four possible causes of *khawāṭir*: (1) God, (2) the Angels, (3) an individual's ego (*nafs*) and (4) Satan. Significantly, since the actions of

1 For a summary and list of further bibliographic sources, see "ʿAydarūs,' in *Encyclopedia of Islam*, ed. J. H. Kramers et al., new edn., Leiden: E. J. Brill, 1954–2002.

2 The most relevant discussions of *khawāṭir* in the context of ʿAydarūs's work are those presented by Abū Ḥāmid al-Ghazālī and by Murtaḍā al-Zabīdī; see Ghazālī, *Iḥyā' ʿulūm al-dīn*, Book XXI: *Kitāb sharḥ ʿajā'ib al-qalb*, trans. Walter J. Skellie as *The Marvels of the Heart*, Louisville, KY: Fons Vitae, 2010 and Zabīdī, *Itḥāf al-sāda al-mutaqqīn bi-sharḥ Iḥyā' ʿulūm al-dīn*, Cairo: al-Maṭbaʿa al-Muyammaniyya, 1311/1894.

all of these entities lie beyond an individual's conscious control, this means that the appearance of *khawāṭir* is also beyond one's conscious control. Consequently, all that a spriritual wayfarer can hope to achieve is to manage one's response to *khawāṭir* through rigorous spiritual training.[1]

Thus, the reason why ʿAydarūs considered it to be so important to understand motivating thoughts and their sources was because the soundness of an individual's actions in the eyes of God depended on the acceptability of the motivating thought that initiated those actions in the first place. For as ʿAydarūs explained, only Lordly and angelic thoughts can 'grow into shoots of felicity,' whereas egotistic and devilish thoughts are doomed to 'grow into shoots of damnation'. His guidance for the seeker therefore focused on two distinct, but related, aspects of training: the first was acquiring sufficient knowledge and understanding in order to distinguish between the four possible sources of *khawāṭir*, and the second was finding practical ways to encourage good motivating thoughts and discourage bad ones. The most important practical methods that he prescribed to counter the negative effects of *khawāṭir* were to practise remembrance (*dhikr*) and retreat (*khalwa*), to act with propriety (*bi-adab*) and to find a spiritual guide (*shaykh*) to help one on the spiritual path. Above all, he stressed that the seeker cannot hope to attain proximity to God without renunciation (*zuhd*) and God-fearingness (*taqwā*), as they are the keys to the spiritual path.

A core element of *The Fragrant Scent* is ʿAydarūs's extensive use of quotations from the Qur'ān and the sayings of the Prophet to present authoritative proof for his explanations and advice concerning the path to God. In combination with accompanying tales

1 In modern psychology, such unconscious influences on a person's behaviour are described in terms of the workings of the 'subconscious' (and more recently, in terms of the implicit processes of cognition). For similar observations concerning the concept of *khawāṭir*, see Samer Akkach, *The Letters of a Sufi Scholar: The Correspondence of ʿAbd al-Ghanī al-Nābulusī (1641–1731)*, Leiden: Brill, 2010, p. 100.

of the Pious Predecessors (*al-Salaf al-Ṣāliḥ*) and the most illustrious early Sufis, this feature of the text enables the reader to not only understand the exemplary conduct of these Knowers of God, but also to embody it by applying it to their own spiritual practice.

THE TRANSLATION

The translation presented here is based on the Arabic edition of the text published by the Royal Aal Al-Bayt Institute for Islamic Thought in Amman, as are the explanatory notes and references that accompany the translation.[1] In order to help the reader navigate the work, section headings have been added to the text of the translation (such as, 'On Motivating Thoughts,' 'On Remembrance,' etc.).

1 Abū al-Marāḥim ʿAbd al-Raḥmān b. Muṣṭafā b. Shaykh al-ʿAydarūs, *al-ʿArf al-ʿāṭir fī maʿrifat al-khawāṭir wa-ghayrihā min al-jawāhir*, Amman: Royal Aal Al-Bayt Institute for Islamic Thought, [no date].

THE FRAGRANT SCENT: ON THE KNOWLEDGE OF MOTIVATING THOUGHTS AND OTHER SUCH GEMS

In the Name of God, the Merciful, the Compassionate. May God's blessings and peace be upon the Messenger of God and upon his household, Companions and the Friends of God.

Introduction

This is a short and refined commentary on some excellent verses of poetry that we have composed and entitled, *The Fragrant Scent: On the Knowledge of Motivating Thoughts and Other Such Gems* (al-ʿArf al-ʿāṭir fī maʿrifat al-khawāṭir wa-ghayrihā min al-jawāhir). May God, the Outwardly Manifest in all loci of manifestation, be exalted above all limitations!

The verses are the following:

Motivating thoughts, my dear, are four,
And they are those whose cases are diverse:
There are those attributed to Satan;
And those that emanate from the ego;
Others are attributed to the action of an Angel,
While the most significant are bestowed by He Who has Dominion.
Thus, O spiritual wayfarer, their enumeration is complete,
So know this and act; that a pitch-black night may be dissipated.

First, I must mention a note of warning in which I resolve any problematic issues that may arise in the course of this short commentary (*taʿlīqa*) regarding the noble Qur'ān and other similar things.

THE QUR'ĀN HAS AN OUTWARD AND AN INWARD MEANING

You should know that it has been firmly established through rigorously authenticated Prophetic sayings (*bi'l-aḥādīth al-ṣaḥīḥa*) that every single verse of the Qur'ān has an outward meaning[1] (*ẓahr*[an])—that is, its well-known and accepted commentary, whose remit should not go beyond what has been transmitted. Indeed, the Messenger of God (may God bless him and grant him peace) referred to it in saying, 'Whoever interprets the Qur'ān through his personal opinion, let him take his seat in the Fire.'[2] It has also been firmly established through rigorously authenticated Prophetic sayings that every single verse of the Qur'ān has an inward meaning (*baṭn*[an]). Its remit is that it does not overstep the Book or the Prophetic *Sunna*, and it should not be stated categorically that this inward meaning of

1 This is part of a Prophetic saying that was narrated by Ibn Ḥibbān in his rigorously authenticated collection; Abū Ḥatim Muḥammad b. Ḥibbān al-Bustī Ibn Ḥibbān, *al-Iḥsān bi-tartīb Ṣaḥiḥ Ibn Ḥibbān*, ed. Kamāl Yūsuf al-Ḥūt, Beirut: Dār al-Kutub al-ʿIlmiyya, 1987, vol. 1, p. 146. The text of this Prophetic saying, which was reported by Ibn Masʿūd, is as follows: 'The Messenger of God (may God bless him and grant him peace) said, "The Qur'ān was revealed according to seven letters; each verse of these has an outward and inward meaning."'

2 Narrated by Tirmidhī; Muḥammad b. ʿĪsā al-Tirmidhī, *Sunan al-Tirmidhī*, ed. Ibrāhīm ʿAṭwah ʿAwwaḍ, Cairo: Dār al-Ḥadīth, [no date], nos. 2950 and 2951. The second of these Prophetic sayings was reported by Ibn ʿAbbās, who related that the Prophet (may God bless him and grant him peace) said, 'Be fearful of God in reporting anything from me except that which you know, for whoever intentionally lies about me, let him take his seat in the Fire; and whoever interprets the Qur'ān through his own personal opinion, let him also take his seat in the Fire.' Tirmidhī stated that the first Prophetic saying was well authenticated/rigorously authenticated (*ḥasan ṣaḥīḥ*) and the second was well authenticated (*ḥasan*); Tirmidhī, '*Wa-min sūrat fātiḥat al-kitāb*' in *Sunan al-Tirmidhī, Kitab Tafsir al-Qur'ān*.

the verse is the only meaning intended and nothing else, for there is a clear difference between such an interpretation and that of the Esotericists (*Bāṭiniyya*).[1] This type of interpretation instead belongs to a form of supported meanings (*min bāb wujūh al-iḥtimālāt*), not by recourse to reason (*lā bi'l-ʿaql*) and without insisting categorically that it is the only intended meaning.

An example of this is the saying of Ibn ʿAbbās (may God be well pleased with father and son and benefit through them) regarding the saying of God Most High, *He sends down water out of heaven, and the wadis flow each in its measure* (Q.XIII.17), said that 'Water, in this verse, means knowledge (*ʿilm*) while *wadis* ('valleys') means the hearts (*qulūb*).' Which is to say that from the heaven of the Divine Presence (*al-ḥaḍra al-ilāhiyya*), God Most High manifests the water of knowledge, and each valley of those hearts receptive to it flows [with this water] into [their] souls (*nufūs*) to the extent of their fullness with this knowledge. This type of interpretation is not inadmissible when there is a shift from the outward to the inward meaning, while at the same time affirming the outward meaning. What is inadmissible is the Esotericists' method of interpretation that completely denies the outward meaning, which amounts to clear disbelief (*kufr*).

In sum, this type of interpretation varies according to the state (*ḥāl*) of the interpreter, in terms of the clarity of his understanding (*ṣafā' al-fahm*), rank of gnosis (*rutbat al-maʿrifa*) and share of closeness (*qurb*) to God Most High. It is in this context that Abū al-Dardā' (may God be pleased with him) said, 'A man does not fully understand until he sees numerous layers of meaning in the Qur'ān.' More amazing than this is the saying of Ibn Masʿūd (may God be well pleased with him), 'There is not a single verse except that it has people who will know it [that is, its correct interpretation].'

Such words from him (may God be pleased with him) instigate each genuine student possessing a lofty resolve to distil the sources

1 *Bāṭiniyya* is a reference to the Ismāʿīlīs.

of speech and understand its minute meanings and the obscure secrets from his heart. Indeed, it was to this that Shaykh Miḥḍār[1] (may God benefit by him) alluded when he said, 'If I so wished, I could dictate the equivalent of one hundred camel-loads [of volumes] regarding the meaning of the words of God Most High, *And for whatever verse We abrogate or cast into oblivion*... (Q.II.106), and its meaning would still not be exhausted.'

Let us go back and finish what we started [to say above]. We say that every single verse of the Qur'ān also has a limit (*ḥadd*), such that textual-based evidence should not be omitted in favour of reason in its outward meaning and in its inward meaning; it should not overstep the grammatical rules of the Arabic language [or] that which is intelligible. Moreover, each verse of the Qur'ān has a place to which one may ascend (*muṭṭalaʿ*)—that is, through it one ascends to that which is beyond commentary (*tafsīr*) and interpretation (*ta'wīl*), until one beholds the Speaker (*Mutakallim*), as was reported from

1 He was the Prophetic descendent, the very learned ʿUmar al-Miḥḍār b. al-Sayyid al-Sharīf ʿAbd al-Raḥmān al-Saqqāf Bā ʿAlawī. Born in Tarim, he was the foremost shaykh of his time who possessed mastery in the method of the People of Sufism (*taṣawwuf*). He memorised the Qur'ān while still very young, as well as Nawawī's *Minhāj al-ṭālibīn* and Sulamī's *Ḥaqā'iq al-taṣawwuf*. He travelled to Shiḥr, Yemen and the two Holy Sanctuaries, and he kept the company of the greatest scholars of his time. He died in 833/1429 and was buried in the Zanbal cemetery in Tarim. See ʿAydarūs b. ʿUmar b. ʿAydarūs al-Ḥabshī, *ʿIqd al-yawāqīt al-jawhariyya wa-simṭ al-ʿayn al-dhahabiyya bi-dhikr ṭarīq al-sādāt al-ʿAlawīyya*, Cairo: al-Maṭbaʿa al-ʿĀmiriyya al-Sharafiyya, 1317/1899, vol. II, p. 121 and Muḥammad b. Abī Bakr Bā ʿAlawī al-Shillī, *al-Mashraʿ al-rawī fī manāqib al-sāda al-kirām Āl Abī ʿAlawī*, Cairo: al-Maṭbaʿa al-ʿĀmiriyya al-Sharafiyya, 1319/1901, vol. II, p. 244.

Imam Jaʿfar al-Ṣādiq[1] (may God be pleased with him and benefit by him), who said, 'God has manifested Himself to His servants in His Speech, but people see not.' It is also reported that he once fainted while performing the prayer. When he was questioned about it, he said, 'I kept repeating the verse until I heard it from the Speaker.'

When the Forelock of Divine Oneness (*Nāṣiyat al-Tawḥīd*) beckons to the Sufi, and he lends his ear to God's promises and threats, ridding himself of everything other than God Most High, he becomes ever-present in a state of contemplation before God and, upon reciting the Qur'ān, sees his tongue (or the tongues of others) like the tree of Moses (peace be upon him) when God made him hear His address to him from it, [saying,] *Verily I am God*. May God bestow this state upon us through His favour! He is indeed Magnanimous and Generous.

Let us now begin what we have intended with the help of Him Who exists and is besought by all. We say, you should know that there are four widely known motivating thoughts (*khawāṭir*): lordly (*rabbānī*), egotistic (*nafsānī*), angelic (*malakī*) and devilish (*shayṭānī*).

1 He was the most distinguished scholar and one of the most illustrious figures of the household of the noble Prophet (may God bless him and grant him peace), our master Abū ʿAbd Allāh Jaʿfar al-Ṣādiq b. Muḥammad al-Bāqir b. ʿAlī Zayn al-ʿĀbidīn b. al-Ḥusayn, the grandson of the Messenger of God (may God bless him and grant him peace) and the son of ʿAlī b. Abī Ṭālib. He was born in Medina in the year 80/699 (83/702 according to some sources). He was one of the most distinguished followers of the Prophetic Companions (*Tābiʿīn*) and one of their greatest scholars. He was given the agnomen, *al-Ṣādiq*, because he never lied. He died in Medina on 15 Rajab 148/6 September 765 and was buried in Baqīʿ cemetery. See Aḥmad b. Muḥammad b. Abī Bakr b. Khallikan, *Wafayāt al-aʿyān wa-anbā' abnā' al-zamān*, ed. Iḥsān ʿAbbās, Beirut: Dār al-Thaqāfa, [no date], vol. I, p. 327; Abū al-Faraj Jamāl al-Din b. al-Jawzī, *Ṣifat al-ṣafwa*, ed. Mahmūd Fākhūrī and Muḥammad Rawās Qalʿajī, Beirut: Dār al-Maʿrifa, 1979, vol. II, pp. 168–174; and Khayr al-Dīn al-Ziriklī, *al-Aʿlām: Qāmūs tarājim li-ashhar al-rijāl wa'l-nisā' min al-ʿarab wa'l-mustaʿribīn wa'l-mustashriqīn*, Beirut: Dār al-ʿIlm li'l-Malāyīn, 1984, vol. II, p. 126.

On Motivating Thoughts

THE IMPORTANCE OF KNOWING MOTIVATING THOUGHTS

Knowledge about motivating thoughts is one of the most important affairs of the servant because a motivating thought is the beginning of an action (*al-khāṭir awwal al-fiʿl*) and its initiation (*muftataḥuhu*). This is because actions stem from thoughts, whereas the servant is only created for worship, which consists of actions. These actions that emanate from thoughts become acts of worship in measure with the soundness of thoughts, and this cannot happen unless one is able to distinguish between them. Distinguishing these thoughts is therefore the first thing that is obligated for the servant after the obligation of knowing the Creator and prophethood. In fact, a scholar (may God have mercy upon him) maintained that the knowledge (*ʿilm*) that is incumbent upon one to seek in compliance with the saying of the Messenger of God (may God bless him and grant him peace), 'Seeking knowledge is an obligation upon every Muslim,'[1] is the knowledge of motivating thoughts (*ʿilm al-khawāṭir*). His reasoning was that motivating thoughts initiate action; meaning that the nullity of the former entails the nullity of the latter.

However, this position is untenable because the Messenger of God (may God bless him and grant him peace) made this [pursuit of knowledge] obligatory for every Muslim, and not all Muslims possess the innate nature (*qarīḥa*) and gnosis (*maʿrifa*) that allows them to know thoughts. The obligation to know thoughts therefore applies to the elites (*khawāṣṣ*) who possess sound and innate natures. The dependence of the soundness of actions on knowledge of thoughts should be understood in terms of fully discerning whether or not they are acceptable; not in terms of their legal capacity.

Once this is known, the student should know that motivating thoughts are like seeds; some of them grow into shoots of felicity (*saʿāda*) and others into shoots of damnation (*shaqāwa*). Those

1 Narrated by Ibn Māja; it is a well-authenticated Prophetic saying.

that grow into shoots of felicity are motivating thoughts from the Abidingly Real (*khāṭir al-Ḥaqq*)—except when one is angry—and [they are] also angelic thoughts (*khāṭir al-malak*). And those that grow into shoots of damnation are egotistic motivating thoughts (*khāṭir al-nafs*)—except when one is in a state of tranquillity—and [they are] also devilish thoughts (*khāṭir al-shayṭān*)—except when Satan intends to deceive one by manifesting good thoughts until he draws the servant to an evil thought, or when he manifests a good thought in order to distract the servant from something that is more important than it.

REASONS FOR THE MISCONCEPTIONS CONCERNING MOTIVATING THOUGHTS

There are four reasons for the misconceptions (*ishtibāh*) concerning motivating thoughts (not five), and when they are removed, one will know [which] motivating thoughts are beneficial (*nāfiʿ*) and [which] are harmful (*ḍārr*). Only then can one seek the former and flee from the latter. The first of these reasons is a weakness of certainty (*yaqīn*) about matters relating to the Afterlife, or about those who report about that. The second is a lack of knowledge through which the attributes of the soul (*ṣifāt al-nafs*) and its character traits (*akhlāqahā*) are known, which is seeking what is beneficial and fleeing from what is harmful. When these are not known, the ego (*nafs*) confuses what is beneficial with what is harmful (and vice versa) as a way of seeking what it desires and avoiding what disagrees with its base desire (*hawāhā*). The third cause is pursuing one's base desire even when one knows that this will cause one to err from God's path (*sabīl Allāh*), and [despite knowing] that, whoever errs from His path will receive a severe chastisement. Even then, the ego may overpower a person to the point where he loses control over it because he has not bridled it by means of God-fearingness (*taqwā*), and has let it be used to indulge its desires. When this happens, the foundations of God-fearingness are unsettled and darkness seeps into the heart (*qalb*). The heart then does not have enough light with which to ward off the darkness of the ego, thus allowing the ego to overpower him. The fourth cause is love of the world (*maḥabbat al-dunyā*) due to its glory and wealth—not inasmuch as it leads a person to desires (*shahawāt*), but because it leads him to seek exultation through riches and status in the eyes of people. The differences between all of these [reasons for misconceptions about motivating thoughts] can be understood from what we have already mentioned.

A distinction may be made between knowledge (*ʿilm*) and certitude (*yaqīn*) by saying that knowledge is an emphatic belief that corresponds to fact, whereas certitude is feeling the coolness of this emphatic belief and its groundedness in one's heart. The difference between, [on the one hand,] pursuing base desire (*hawā*) or love of this world (*maḥabbat al-dunyā*), and, [on the other,] the character traits of the soul (*akhlāq al-nafs*), lies in the fact that character traits are the principles of actions, whereas pursuance is itself an action. The difference between pursuing base desire and love of this world lies in the fact that the lover of this world may toil and shun food and sex for its sake, just as he might enjoy status and not find any joy in food or sex.

Whoever has been spared from these four [reasons] becomes strong in faith (*qawīy al-dīn*) and perfected in his knowledge (*kāmil al-maʿrifa*) of the ego and its character traits. He has bridled his ego through God-fearingness (*taqwā*) and has perfected his renunciation (*zuhd*) in this world, with all its wealth and glory. Moreover, after firstly distinguishing between the inspiration of the Angels (*lammat al-malak*) and the whispering of Satan (*lammat al-shayṭān*), he has then ended up knowing the motivating thoughts of the ego and the motivating thoughts of the Abidingly Real.

Whoever has been afflicted by all of these matters does not recognise motivating thoughts, or seek them, out because he does not have a firm enough belief in matters of the Afterlife to seek knowledge of that which is beneficial and that which is harmful [in terms of] the Hereafter (and [it should be noted that] what is beneficial and what is harmful is only considered in relation to matters of the Afterlife by the People of Truth); although he is ignorant of the true nature of what the ego seeks, wrongly thinking that everything that the ego seeks is beneficial and that everything it flees from is harmful, even then, base desire compels him to that, and love of this world [also] helps him to that end, which is the root of all sin.

KNOWLEDGE OF THE SOUL

The unveiling (*inkishāf*) of some motivating thoughts to the exclusion of others is due to the existence of some of these four things and the absence of others. The most mindful of people in the assessment of motivating thoughts (*taqwīm al-khawāṭir*) is also the most mindful in the knowledge of the soul (*maʿrifat al-nafs*). Knowledge of the soul is extremely difficult. It can scarcely be acquired unless one reaches the utmost [degree of] renunciation and God-fearingness. It is for this reason that the Prophet (may God bless him and grant him peace) linked knowledge of God with knowledge of the soul when he said, 'Whoever knows his soul knows his Lord.'[1] This is like linking knowledge of the day with knowledge of the night, for were it not for the onset of night, the merit of the day would remain unknown. Likewise, were it not for knowledge of the soul, the station of servanthood (*maqām*

1 This saying was mentioned by the *Ḥadīth* master Muḥammad b. ʿAbd al-Raḥmān al-Sakhāwī, in his *al-Maqāsid al-ḥasana fī bayān kathīr min al-aḥādīth al-mushtahara ʿalā al-alsina*, ed. Muḥammad ʿUthmān al-Khisht, Beirut: Dār al-Kitab al-ʿArabī, 1985, p. 490, *ḥadīth* no. 1149. It was related from Abū al-Muẓaffar al-Samʿānī that he said, 'This saying is not known as being attributable to the Prophet (may God bless him and grant him peace). Rather, it is attributed to Yaḥyā b. Muʿādh al-Rāzī.' Imam al-Nawawī also mentioned that this saying could not be established as a Prophetic saying, while Mulla ʿAlī al-Harawī al-Makkī al-Qāri' included it as a fabricated saying in his collection of forged sayings entitled, *al-Maṣnūʿ fī maʿrifat al-ḥādīth al-mawḍūʿ*, ed. ʿAbd al-Fattāḥ Abū Ghudda, Aleppo: al-Matbūʿāt al-Islamiyya, 1994, p. 189.

al-ʿubūdiyya) would not be known and, a priori, nor would the station of Lordship (*maqām al-Rubūbiyya*) be fully known either. Despite the utter purity of his soul, the Messenger of God (may God bless him and grant him peace) was always indigent before his Lord by seeking refuge in Him from its evil. He used to say, '[O God!] Do not consign me to my ego (*nafsī*) for [even] the blink of an eye, and protect me the way a newborn baby is protected.'[1] That is, protect me the way a caring parent protects his child, lest it be taken or snatched away by others. When Shaykh ʿAydarūs[2] (may God benefit by him) realised the station of Muḥammadan inheritance (*al-wirātha al-Muḥammadiyya*) from his grandfather (may God bless him and grant him peace), he used to say, 'I am the servant of God who is in need of Him at every breath.'

When the seeker becomes convinced of this lack, he is in fact following the Prophet (may God bless him and grant him peace) in his most eminent station, which is seeing the essential evil of the ego (*sharr al-nafs al-dhātī*) in the station of the soul's tranquillity and perfected traits. This is because that which is [part of] the essence (*mā bi'l-dhāt*) [of the seeker] cannot be completely removed by [anything] other [than God]. This is a refined and subtle insight that is only revealed to he who possesses such perfect gnosis (*maʿrifa*) that he is not deluded by anything manifested of the soul's traits or whatever is obedient to it.

1 The first part of this Prophetic saying was narrated by Ḥākim Naysābūrī and is well authenticated; see Abū ʿAbd Allāh al-Ḥākim al-Naysābūrī, *al-Mustadrak ʿalā al-ṣaḥiḥayn wa-bi-dhaylihi talkhīṣ al-mustadrak li'l-Dhahabī*, Riyadh: Maktabat al-Maʿārif, [no date], vol. I, p. 730. As for its addendum, I could not trace it.

2 He was the Prophetic descendent ʿAbd Allāh b. Abī Bakr b. ʿAbd al-Raḥmān al-Saqqāf, better known as al-ʿAydarūs. He was born in the city of Tarim in the year 811/1408. He studied under a group of jurisprudents and Sufis and excelled in three of the disciplines of the Sacred Law: Qur'ānic exegesis, *Ḥadīth* and Islamic law. Scores of students graduated at his hands. He was the author of numerous books. In the year 865/1460, he died at the age of 54 on the Shahar road and was buried in Tarim. See Ḥabshī, *ʿIqd al-yawāqīt*, vol. II, pp. 118–119.

THE GREATEST DEFECTS OF THE EGO

One of the greatest defects of the ego (*āfāt al-nafs*), as far as the seeker is concerned, is that it may claim extinction (*fanā'*) and subsistence (*baqā'*) through God when the soul is shaken, even though both are characteristics and capabilities of the heart (*qalb*). In such a case, the soul is lying in its claim because it has no existence whatsoever when extinction or subsistence take place; and if it has no existence, how can it [then] lay claim to them?

What really happens here though is that the seeker becomes confused, thinking that his actions, words and movements are through God, and thus he attributes his own actions to Him. We seek refuge in God from ever doing this! This is where he is afflicted by the rising up of the ego and its cloaking [of itself] without him feeling that; instead, he imagines that he is at the station of the heart (*maqām al-qalb*) and [that] his enlightenment is by means of the light of the spirit (*bi-nūr al-rūḥ*). [Only] then does the danger of that become apparent to him. Such confusion only happens to the Masters of Hearts (*Arbāb al-Qulūb*) and the Masters of Spiritual States (*Arbāb al-Aḥwāl*) when they are returned back to the station of the soul (*maqām al-nafs*) without them being aware of it, or when their souls eavesdrop on [their] hearts and, consequently, become uplifted before they are returned, unaware, to their souls.

THE PERFECTED ONES AND THE DEFECTS OF THE EGO

As for the Perfected Ones (*Kummal*), they are immune to this because they cannot claim such a thing for their egos. Rather, this is a slip [that is] exclusively characteristic of those mentioned above, who claim divinity for their egos, [who] attribute their actions to God even though their hearts have not been revitalised by Divine Light, and [who] have not even become intoxicated by [their] spiritual state so as to be excused from this allegation.

It is related that Shiblī said, 'I have drunk from the same goblet as Ḥallāj, but I became sober whereas Ḥallāj remained drunk.'[1] When [news of] this reached Ḥallāj, he said, 'Had he drunk from the same goblet as I, he would have remained drunk just as I have.'[2] When this exchange between the two of them reached Junayd,[3] he said, 'We give precedence to the words of a sober person over those of a drunk'; and so he gave precedence to the spiritual state (*ḥāl*) of Shiblī over that of Ḥallāj.

It is for this reason that it was said that most ecstatic utterances (*shaṭḥ*) are the result of a state of spiritual drunkenness (*min sukr al-ḥāl*) and the overpowering might of ultimate spiritual reality (*ghalabat sulṭān al-ḥaqīqa*). Hence, whoever is completely sober and free from any remnants of drunkenness, and [who] has had calm

1 The ancestors of Abū Bakr (or Dulf) b. Jaḥdar al-Shiblī hailed from Khorasan. Shiblī was born in Samarra in the year 247/861. He was famous for his righteousness and God-fearingness. He kept the company of Junayd as well as a number of illustrious masters of his time. He studied *Ḥadīth* and followed the Mālikī school of jurisprudence. Many poems attributed to him have been printed as a collection. He lived to the ripe old age of 87 and died in 334/945. He was buried in the Khayzarān cemetery in Baghdad. See ʿAbd al-Wahhāb b. ʿAlī al-Shaʿrānī, *al-Ṭabaqāt al-kubrā*, Cairo: Maktabat Muṣṭafā al-Bābī al-Ḥalabī, 1954, vol. I, pp. 103–105; Khalīl b. Aybak b. ʿAbd Allāh al-Ṣafadī, *al-Wāfī bi'l-wafayāt*, ed. Helmut Ritter et al., Weisbaden: Franz Steiner, 1983–2005, vol. XIV, p. 25; and Ziriklī, *al-Aʿlām*, vol. II, p. 341.

2 Abū Mughīth al-Ḥusayn b. Mansūr al-Ḥallāj was raised in Wāsiṭ in Iraq, then moved to Basra. He was considered to be one of the greatest ascetics and devotees. He kept the company of great masters of Sufism such as Junayd, Nūrī, ʿAmr b. ʿUthmān al-Makkī, al-Fūṭī and others. He was executed during the reign of the Abbasid ruler Muqtadir in Dhū al-Qiʿda 309/March 922, after being denounced by his opponents. See Shaʿrānī, *al-Ṭabaqāt al-kubrā*, vol. I, pp. 107–109; Ṣafadī, *al-Wāfī bi'l-wafayāt*, vol. XIII, pp. 70–75; and Ziriklī, *al-Aʿlām*, vol. II, p. 260.

3 Abū al-Qāsim al-Junayd b. Muḥammad b. al-Junayd al-Baghdādī al-Khazzār. His father was from Nahāwand but he was born in Baghdad. Scholars consider him the master of Sufism par excellence, because he laid his doctrine on the basis of the Book and the *Sunna*. He was a distinguished jurisprudent and delivered legal edicts when he was twenty years old. He died in 297/909 and was buried in Baghdad. See Ibn Khallikān, *Wafayāt al-aʿyān*, vol. I, p. 373; Shaʿrānī, *al-Ṭabaqāt al-kubrā*, vol. I, p. 84; and Ziriklī, *al-Aʿlām*, vol. II, p. 141.

(*sakīna*) descend upon his heart, will veil the ultimate spiritual reality by means of [his] knowledge (*bi'l-ʿilm*) and will bind [himself] with the limits of servanthood. So know this—for its knowledge is rare indeed—because knowledge of it clears away all the confusions that remain concealed from most Masters of Hearts. ʿAbd Allāh b. al-Mubārak[1] (may God benefit through him) said regarding the words of God Most High, *And struggle for God as is His due* (Q.xxii.78): 'This refers to struggling against the ego (*mujāhadat al-nafs*) and base desire (*hawā*).' This is true *jihād*, the greatest *jihād*, according to the report from the Messenger of God (may God bless him and grant him peace), who, upon returning from one of his military expeditions, said, 'We have returned from the lesser *jihād* to the greater *jihād*.'[2]

THE EGO IS THE GREATEST ENEMY

The ego is indeed the greatest enemy (*al-ʿadūw al-akbar*) within you. All of the harms of this enemy work against you. [Waging] *jihād* against the unbelievers was only prescribed to avert the harms that they could inflict upon the Muslims who worship God; however, the ego is a greater stumbling block than the disbelievers, because it is the greatest enemy. It has craving needs and diverse desires that drag one to the abyss of total destruction. Despite this, it is not permissible to destroy it, as it is a mount; nor is it permissible to leave it to its own devices. Rather, it is necessary to bridle

1 Imam Abū ʿAbd al-Raḥmān b. ʿAbd Allāh b. al-Mubārak b. Wāḍiḥ al-Ḥanẓalī al-Tamīmī al-Marūzī was born in the year 118/736 and lived in Khorasan. He travelled a great deal for trade, in order to perform the Pilgrimage and as a fighter for the sake of God. He was the author of several books. He died on his return from fighting the Byzantines in the year 181/797 and was buried in the city of Hīt on the shores of the Euphrates. See Ibn Khallikān, *Wafayāt al-aʿyān*, vol. iii, pp. 32–33; Ṣafadī, *al-Wāfī bi'l-wafayāt*, vol. xvii, p. 419; Shaʿrānī, *al-Ṭabaqāt al-kubrā*, vol. i, pp. 59–60; and Ziriklī, *al-Aʿlām*, vol. iv, p. 115.

2 Narrated by Bayhaqī in *Kitāb al-Zuhd* and by Khaṭīb Baghdādī in his *Ta'rīkh Baghdād*. The *Ḥadīth* master Aḥmad b. al-Ṣiddīq al-Ghumārī stated in his *al-Mudāwī li-ʿilal al-jāmiʿ al-ṣaghīr* that this Prophetic saying was well authenticated.

it by means of God-fearingness, and to restrain it from its diverse needs and desires that are only known to a few singular Realised Ones (*Muḥaqqiqīn*), who are adept at dealing with it.

HOW TO SLAY THE EGO

It is necessary to struggle against the ego (*nafs*) by means of that which gives it a new death at every instant. It is to this that the Messenger (may God bless him and grant him peace) alluded when he said, 'Die before you die',[1] and to which Shaykh ʿAbd al-Qādir al-Jīlānī alluded in saying, 'I died a thousand deaths', and also Shaykh Abū Bakr al-ʿAydarūs[2] in his ode (*muwashshaḥ*): 'For Your sake, I was killed a thousand times / Before even tasting [physical] death.'

One should also remind one's ego that the desires of this world are like poisoned sweets. In fact, they are more detrimental [even] than that, as revealed to the Knowers of God (*li'l-ʿĀrifīn bi'Llāh*). Their effect on one's religion is like the effect of poison on the body. So how can any intelligent person indulge in them?

One should also remind one's ego that even if it were to miss [out on] all of the pleasures of this world, no great harm would come to it because they are ephemeral and [have] dire, lasting consequences. In this world, it is difficult for it [the ego] to bear an

1 In his book, *al-Maqāsid al-ḥasana*, the *Ḥadīth* master Sakhāwī, reporting from his teacher, the *Ḥadīth* master Ibn Ḥajar, stated that this saying was not established as attributable to the Messenger of God. In his *al-Asrār al-marfūʿa fī al-akhbār al-mawdūʿa*, Shaykh Mulla ʿAlī al-Qāri' stated the following: 'I say, this is of the sayings of the Sufis. It means, die voluntarily before your real eventual death. What is meant by voluntary death is abstention from desires and distractions and what these entail by way of slips and heedlessness.'

2 Abū Bakr b. ʿAbd Allāh al-ʿAydarūs b. Abī Bakr b. ʿAbd al-Raḥmān al-Saqqāf was born in the city of Tarim in the year 851/1447. He memorised the Qur'ān while still very young and he studied with his father as well as with some of the greatest scholars of his time. He moved to Aden in 889/1484 and remained there until his death in the year 914/1508. He was buried in the well-known Qaṭīʿ cemetery. See Shillī, *al-Mashraʿ al-rawī*, vol. II, pp. 34–41 and Ḥabshī, *ʿIqd al-yawāqīt*, vol. II, pp. 117–118.

ant's bite, much less being whipped or cauterised—even though these only cause finite pains. So how will it bear iron hooks in the Afterlife, [or] being handled by harsh, ruthless Angels, [or] being burned inwardly and outwardly, or being bitten by serpents the size of camels and scorpions the size of mules—all created from the Fire, non-stop and forever? In fact, blameworthy character traits themselves will turn into serpents and scorpions in the Afterlife. It was indeed to this that the Prophet (may God bless him and grant him peace) alluded in his saying, 'These are your works given back to you.'[1]

By scaring the ego in this manner, it will melt just as iron melts with fire. This is because fear (*khawf*), qua fear, is hot. One should give the ego the good news that all acts of obedience (*ṭāʿāt*) are beneficial in the Afterlife, just as money is beneficial in this world. One should also give it the good news that if it were to turn towards (*idhā tawajjahat ilā*) God Most High, it would join the souls of the Knowers of God Most High, whose spirits circumambulate the Throne of the Essence (*ʿArsh al-Dhāt*), whose hearts receive support of overflowing goodness from their spirits by means of the latter's emanation, and whose hearts spill emanations upon their souls from this, because their egos' desire has turned away from the Lower World (*al-ʿĀlam al-Suflī*) and redirected [itself] to the Higher World (*al-ʿĀlam al-ʿUlwī*). So much so that they consider the hardships [that] they eventually encounter to be sweeter than worldly pleasures. Thus, they do not care for ephemeral desires, just as a chess player does not care for food or sex when the joy of the game overpowers him. This is because it is an inward joy (*ladhdha bāṭiniyya*) that overcomes outward joys, even though such

1 Narrated by Abū Nuʿaym al-Iṣbahānī in his *Ḥilyat al-awliyā' wa-ṭabaqāt al-aṣfiyā'*. In his authentication of the Prophetic sayings mentioned in Ghazālī's *Iḥyā'*, the *Ḥadīth* master ʿIrāqī stated that this saying was narrated by Ṭabarānī in his *Awsaṭ* and by Ḥākim Naysābūrī in his *al-Mustadrak* with a weak chain of transmission; see Abū Ḥāmid Muḥammad b. Muḥammad al-Ghazālī, *Iḥyā' ʿulūm al-dīn*, Beirut: Dār al-Maʿrifa, [no date].

a joy is ephemeral, whereas the joy of the souls of the Knowers of God is lasting, and can never be compared to it.

One should also remind the ego of the things that God has prepared for His beloved ones in the Garden of Eden: that which no eye has seen, no ear has heard and which has never occurred to the minds of mortals. The joy of beholding God's Noble Countenance (*Wajh Allāh al-Karīm*) is the greatest of all joys. Upon such a reminder, the ego gradually acquires tranquillity and finds solace; otherwise, its dominance over one is not an excuse, as it has no power over one save through that which has made it greedy.

THE CAUSE OF LOVE OF THE EGO

As for the ego's advancing [the claim that] destiny (*qadar*) is an excuse for it to commit acts of disobedience, this is even worse than the acts of disobedience it commits, as pointed out by the Knowers of God Most High. You should know that the faults of the ego are concealed from most people because the ego is a beloved enemy (*ʿadūw maḥbūb*), and he who is in love is blind to the faults of his beloved, such that he does not see any of those faults. With love (*maḥabba*), no faults are seen. However, faults are also difficult to see because of the difficult nature of the ego. The Spiritual Pole (*Quṭb*) ʿAydarūs (may God benefit through him) said, 'The Sufis are unanimous that there is no veil between the servant (*ʿabd*) and his Lord (*wa-rabbihi*) except his ego.' May God protect us through His power from its evil! Amen. It is in this context that God Most High said to one of His beloved ones, 'Leave your ego and then come!'

THE DIFFERENCE BETWEEN THE EGO'S MISGIVINGS AND SATAN'S WHISPERINGS

You should also know that the Knowers of God (may God be well pleased with them and benefit through them) have differentiated between the misgivings of the ego (*hawājis al-nafs*), which are its motivating thoughts that demand its share of things, and the whispering of Satan (*wasāwis al-shayṭān*), even though both are accomplices in evil. It is said that when the ego projects a motivating thought in the pursuit of something, it persists with this thought until it obtains what it wants, never accepting anything else in its stead. By contrast, when Satan whispers a contravention to a person, and this person does not respond, Satan moves on and whispers another sin [to him] without ever insisting on the first sin or the second. This is because his intention is not to insist that a person engages in one particular sin to the exclusion of others, but rather to tempt one in whatever way he can, so when he fails with one whisper, he tries another.

By way of analogy, the difference between a motivating thought inspired by the Abidingly Real (*khāṭir al-Ḥaqq*) and that which is inspired by an Angel (*khāṭir al-Malak*) lies in [the fact] that the Angel's aim is guidance (*irshād*). So when one inspired motivating thought fails to guide a servant, he inspires another, whereas the Abidingly Real casts down a thought and then insists on it due to His knowledge of the servant's righteousness (*ṣalāḥ al-ʿabd*) and because of His solicitude (*ʿināyatihi*) towards him. However, God's insistence is unlike that of the ego, for when His inspired thought fails, He inspires another one.

The Knowers of God (may God be well pleased with them) have also spoken about the eventuality of two motivating thoughts being inspired by the Abidingly Real, where both are inspired thoughts to do good acts, and there is an insistence on both. Which of the two thoughts is to be followed in this case, the first or the second? In answer, it was said that one should follow the first thought because it is inspired by the Abidingly Real and must necessarily last until the occurrence of the second thought, and the third, and so on; so it becomes the locus of contemplation (*maḥall al-ta'ammul*) whereby one acquires divine knowledge.

By contrast, there is not much contemplation about the second inspired thought, so there is no action upon it, because the condition of knowledge is contemplation. However, it has also been said that one should follow the second thought. This is because when one is inspired with the first, one becomes enlightened by it but does not act upon it due to detecting a special dispensation (*rukhṣa*) in it, and being a man of strict resolve, he is stronger with the light of the first.

Another answer suggests that it is fine to follow either the first or the second, for just as it is possible that the second thought is a [form of] strictness, it is also possible that it is a special dispensation [granted] due to seeing the weakness of the servant upon the occurrence of the first thought. So there is no giving of preference to [one over the other] on the basis of precedence, nor is there any need to make a distinction between them as to which one is [a form of] strictness, so [the thought] goes away, or as to which of them is a special dispensation, so [the thought] leaves. This is because it may well be that what is intended by the first thought is gentleness, so special dispensation in this case is more appropriate than strictness because special dispensation may be followed by a spiritual insight of happiness or elation, whereas strictness may be followed by a spiritual insight of sadness or constriction.

SPIRITUAL INSIGHTS ARE MORE GENERAL THAN MOTIVATING THOUGHTS

The Knowers of God (may God sanctify their secrets) have stated that spiritual insights (*wāridāt*) are more general than motivating thoughts. This is because, being an inner mode of expression (*kalām*^{an} *nafsiyy*^{an}), thoughts are connected to the essence of the person who has them by means of a kind of speech (*bi-naw*^{c} *khiṭāb*) that concerns the person who has the motivating thoughts, or which concerns something other than him or something demanded of him. Spiritual insights, on the other hand, consist of everything that descends upon the heart from the Abidingly Real, [regardless of] whether they are thoughts or something else, such as the spiritual insight of happiness (*wārid al-surūr*) upon beholding beauty, the spiritual insight of sadness (*wārid al-ḥuzn*) upon beholding rigour, the spiritual insight of constriction (*wārid al-qabḍ*) upon the expectation of being veiled (*ḥijāb*), and the spiritual insight of elation (*wārid al-basṭ*) when expecting unveiling (*kashf*).

By means of the light of Divine Oneness (*bi-nūr al-Tawḥīd*), the seeker accepts thoughts from God Most High because when he is overwhelmed by Divine Oneness, he draws closer to the All-Conquering One (*al-Wāḥid al-Qahhār*). Thus, it has been said that thoughts are from the light of Divine Oneness, which is disclosed to the seeker's spirit; and by means of the light of gnosis (*bi-nūr al-maʿrifa*) the seeker accepts thoughts from the Angels. For upon possessing gnosis, he acquires an affinity with heavenly intellects and souls (*al-ʿuqūl wa'l-nufūs al-samāwiyya*), and joins the Angels. By means of the light of faith (*bi-nūr al-īmān*)—that is, by the light of insight (*bi-nūr al-baṣīra*)—the heart rejects the direction of the soul. This is because the soul longs for the vileness of egotistic desires, and with its (that is, the soul's) indulgence in this vileness, the real pleasures are missed. By means of the light of Islam (*bi-nūr al-Islām*)—that is, the outward injunctions of the Sacred Law—the enemy is repelled, and he is none other than Satan.

THE PERFECTED AND THE UNPERFECTED ONES ON THE SPIRITUAL PATH

All of this concerns the Perfected One who has grasped the verities of renunciation (*ḥaqā'iq al-zuhd*), such that his insight has become illumined, his gnosis has become limpid and he has ended up in the World of Divine Oneness (*ʿĀlam al-Tawḥīd*). As for the unperfected seeker, who is the one who falls short of apprehending the verities of renunciation—much less what is higher, such as illumined inner sight, limpid gnosis and ending up in the World of Divine Oneness—he should first weigh [his] motivating thoughts on the scale of the Sacred Law. If it is something obligatory (*farḍ*) or recommended (*mandūb*), he should accept it, and if it is forbidden (*muḥarram*) or offensive (*makrūh*), he should reject it. When two thoughts are equal due to them both being legally indifferent (*mubāḥ*), then after a thorough contemplation of his ego's inherent desire, he should accept the one that is closer of the two to opposing the base desire of his ego. He should always believe that his ego is never free from this, for as long as [any] aspect of base desire is not clear to him, he should not go ahead with any of his thoughts.

Indeed, the ego may have an inherent base desire (*hawan kāmin*) regarding one of two thoughts, which must be the lower of the [two] matters on account of its affinity with it. This is because the predominant trait of the ego is crookedness due to its tendency to veer towards that which is low like itself. This is why one poet wrote: 'When two matters are obscure, then the best one is that which, / If you were to undertake [it], the ego would find it heavy.'

THE OBFUSCATIONS OF THE EGO AND HOW TO DIFFERENTIATE THEM

It often happens that the ego obfuscates its inherent base desire through the eagerness of the heart (*bi-nashāṭ al-qalb*) to the extent that a motivating thought prompting one to perform an act of worship may be received with eagerness by the ego because of the ego's inherent base desire. And that is due to what is within it in terms of conceitedness (*ʿujb*), showing off (*riyā'*) [and] other diseases of the soul.

Unsuspecting, the servant thinks that this has happened because of the rising up of his heart, deceived as he is by being prompted to engage in an act of worship. An example of this is that a servant might feel the spirit, when emerging from his retreat (*min khalwatihi*), to go out into the wilderness or fields, finding it easy to make remembrance (*dhikr*), to contemplate (*fikr*) and to perform all the other endeavours of the heart. He might think that this is due to the goodness of his heart (*min ṭībat al-qalb*) when it is far from being so. Had it been so, he would not have been affected once he returned to his retreat, as we shall later explain. In fact, all of this is due to the eagerness of the ego, even though at the time, it seemed to be from the goodness of the heart because of the ego's obfuscation. The reason that it seemed to him to be from the goodness of the heart at the time is that the ego is expanded (*tanfasiḥu*) due to its emergence from the strictures of retreat and widens through attaining its goal—which is facilitating its base desire by going out into the wilderness or fields, and sightseeing across their open space, [looking at] trees and other sights.

And when the soul (*nafs*) has been widened, it has distanced [itself] from the heart and has withdrawn from its harm and its attraction to its base desires; yet it gazes at what its base desire has attached to in what it sees in the wilderness, so the heart seeks rest from harm [that comes from the soul]. At that time, it is not [harmed] by the wilderness itself, but rather due to the fact that his soul has been attached to gazing at what is in the wilderness, so it [the soul] distances [itself] from it [the heart] so as not to be harmed by it. This is why invocations and thoughts come easily and clearly to him.

This seeking of rest (*tarawwuḥ*) distances the ego because of its heaviness upon the servant when he turns to his dealings with God. In which case, the person is like someone from whom a doltish companion has departed, for as long as this companion stays away, the person remains relaxed. Likewise, as long as the servant is out in the wilderness or fields, he remains relaxed; but when he returns to his retreat and opens the course of his dealings with God—differentiating between his state then and his state while he was in the wilderness or fields—he finds that the ego is connected to the heart because it was keeping its distance from it [the heart] due to walking through the wilderness. So when he returned from out there, the ego returned with added heaviness, which caused the heart to be weary of it more than its initial weariness, since the heart's turbidity is commensurate with the heaviness of the ego. The heart is always weary with that which makes it turbid, because turbidity (*kudūra*) is contrary to the purity (*ṣafā'*) that constitutes its very nature (*ṭabʿihi*).

The reason for the ego's heaviness upon returning from the wilderness is that it was engaged in its base desire while out there, and this makes it harder and stronger. So it seems then that going out into the wilderness was the source of the malady on account of what resulted from it. The servant had initially thought that his malady was the heart's seeking of rest, not that it was the eagerness of the ego. But after his return to his retreat, the error of his thinking became evident to him, even though it had been concealed from him [before]. For had the servant been steadfast in remaining alone in the place of his retreat and had not gone out into the wilderness, then his ego would have increased in its dissolution (*la-zādat nafsuhu dhawbān*^{an}) by forging its base desire, and it would have become lighter. And the lighter it becomes, the subtler it is; and the more subtle it becomes, the more it becomes a righteous companion to the heart, which consequently no longer finds it heavy.

Seeking rest through travel is analogous to seeking rest by going out into the wilderness (which ultimately appeared to be the source of the malady), as it may appear to be like this unless one knows with a certain special knowledge (*bi-ʿilm khāṣṣ yaqīnī*) that a motivating thought [about] travelling, or other similar things, is not from the ego. In which case, one should proceed with it with good intention, asking God to protect one from one's ego.

THE HEART'S QUIET CAPITULATION TO THE EGO

The [kind of] motivating thought discussed above may be due to the awakening of the heart just as the servant thinks, but it is a heart that deceives its master by remaining calm in the face of the ego, and by concealing this from its master. One of the Knowers of God (may God sanctify his secret) said, 'For the last twenty years, my heart has not quietly capitulated to my ego even for a single moment.' If the heart had not quietly capitulated to the ego, then this knower's negation of such a capitulation would not make any sense. For from the quiet capitulation of the heart to the ego, there emanate thoughts resembling lordly thoughts that invite one to expansiveness (*bi'l-siʿa*), even though the time for it has not yet come. But this is concealed from he who has little knowledge and does not recognise the time of expansiveness. This is why no one except scholars who are thoroughly versed in the knowledge of the soul (*ʿilm al-nafs*) and its attributes (*ṣifātihā*) can grasp the heart's hypocrisy regarding the thought emanating from its quiet capitulation to the ego, to the extent that [these scholars] are able to distinguish between the time of expansiveness and the time of necessity on account of their being thoroughly versed in this knowledge.

Most of the defects (*āfāt*) that enter into the Masters of Hearts (*Arbāb al-Qulūb*), who bring a share of certitude along with perfect awareness and spiritual states, are due to the paucity of their knowledge of the soul, to the extent that it is confused with the heart, and due to the paucity of their knowledge of the heart and its quiet capitulation to the soul. This may be explained by [the fact that] a share of base desire remains in the heart and soul. As for the soul, this remainder is due to its very essence, whereas in the heart it is due to its quiet capitulation to the ego. Thus, the origin of this confusion (*ishtibāh*) is the remnant of base desire remaining in both the heart and soul. The servant must therefore know categorically that as long as there remains [even] a vestige of base desire—no matter how slight or subtle it may be—motivating thoughts will always be confused as far as he is concerned. This is because the soul is confused with the heart, and the heart tends to incline towards the soul through the intermediary [of this remnant].

When the ego is completely nullified, it has no business in assimilating the heart by way of concealment, in which case the heart does not quietly capitulate to the ego (*nafs*) but [rather] to the spirit (*rūḥ*). And when this confusion is of the utmost difficulty—to the extent that no one can dispel it except those scholars who are firmly grounded—those who get it wrong should be treated with compassion, especially if they have very little knowledge of the soul and heart. They should not be taken to task for proceeding with the thoughts emanating from the ego when they confuse them as being thoughts of the heart (or thoughts of the heart when it has quietly capitulated to the ego), as long as there is no clear legally mandated reason to do so.

On the other hand, there is no excuse for the person to whom the secrets of the soul and heart are revealed, and who is further privy to a hidden method by means of which he is able to make a distinction between the two when he gets it wrong because of hastiness—either by confusing the ego with the heart, or by not being able to detect the heart's quiet capitulation to the ego.

THE DIRECTIONS FROM WHENCE MOTIVATING THOUGHTS ARRIVE

It is said that each of the four different motivating thoughts has a particular direction (*jiha*) from whence it comes upon the heart. Thus, the motivating thought from the soul (*nafs*) is felt from the regions of the heart (*min arāḍī al-qalb*) because the heart lies midway between the spirit and the soul: the spirit being heavenly, from the World of Command (*ʿĀlam al-Amr*), while the soul is lowly, being from the World of Creation (*ʿĀlam al-Khalq*). The motivating thought emanating from the Abidingly Real (*Ḥaqq*) is felt from above the heart (*min fawq al-qalb*) because God Most High is above all; although, in this case, the projection of the motivating thought is first onto the spirit (*rūḥ*), which is above the heart. The motivating thought from the Angel (*Malak*) is felt from the right side of the heart (*ʿan yamīn al-qalb*) because the Angel lies on the right side of the heart, it being a strong and otherworldly location. The motivating thought from Satan (*shayṭān*) is felt from the left side of the heart (*ʿan yasār al-qalb*) because Satan lies on its left, it being a weak and worldly location.

THE IMPACT OF THE LIGHT OF REMEMBRANCE ON SATAN

What has been mentioned above regarding feeling each of the four different motivating thoughts from a particular direction only applies to a servant who has dissolved his ego through God-fearingness and renunciation until his entire inward aspect (*bāṭinihi*) and outward aspect (*ẓāhirihi*) become pure. Due to this purity, his outward aspect and inward aspect acquire uprightness (*istiqāma*), and so everything falls into its specified place. If it were not for such uprightness, Satan would come from all directions, [just] as he said, *Then I shall come on them from before them and from behind them, from their right hands and their left hands; thou wilt not find most of them thankful* (Q.vii.17). And even upon determining the distinction [between the different directions from whence motivating thoughts come], without purity one would not know from whence Satan comes to one.

When there is purity, though, the servant's heart becomes like a polished mirror such that Satan does not come upon him from any direction without [the servant] perceiving him. [This is] because no other place is left for [Satan] to fit into due to the servant being occupied by that through which he becomes particularly distinguished upon acquiring uprightness from his attributes. But Satan still has a place despite the servant's uprightness, because the latter may succumb to heedlessness, which will allow Satan to have a chance, but the servant often perceives him with the slightest remembrance. God Most High says, *The God-fearing, when a visitation of Satan troubles them, remember, and then see clearly* (Q.vii.17).

Remembrance (*dhikr*) entails light (*nūr*), and light entails seeing (*ibṣār*). Satan wards off the light of remembrance just as one of us wards off fire. The Prophet (may God bless him and grant him peace) said, 'The remembrance of God Most High concerning

Satan is like a gangrenous sore concerning the son of Adam.'[1] It is also said that when remembrance is deeply rooted in the heart, Satan swoons whenever he nears it, so other devils gather around him and enquire as to what has happened to him, and they are told that he has been touched by a human being.

Due to the tremendousness of the secret of remembrance (*sirr al-dhikr*), when a wayfarer imagines that he has consumed unlawful or doubtful food (and the case is as he has imagined) and then occupies himself with remembrance, then after that the secret of remembrance will efface the effects of all that. So know this, for it will benefit you in this blessed time. However, when the servant's whole heart is so blackened that rust tops it, the servant will not see Satan in the first place, whether he comes to him from one particular location or not, and he will be utterly confused as well. This happens when God-fearingness and renunciation have not been perfected, as the Prophet (may God bless him and grant him peace) said, 'When the servant commits a sin, a black spot is dotted on his heart. If he desists, asks forgiveness and repents, then the black dot is removed. If he returns to sinning, more black spots will be dotted on his heart until rust tops it.'[2] God Most High has said, *No indeed; but that they were earning has rusted upon their hearts* (Q. LXXXIII.14).

What is incumbent upon the servant is that he should immediately seek repentance (*tawba*) after falling into sin, otherwise his

1 Narrated by Daylamī in *Musnad al-Firdaws* from the report of Ibn ʿAbbās as attributable to the Prophet (may God bless him and grant him peace). Its chain of transmission includes al-ʿAlā' b. Maslama who is accused of forging *Ḥadīths*. This saying was also narrated by Abū Nuʿaym in *Ta'rīkh Aṣbahān*, who attributed it to Kaʿb, but its authenticity is not established.

2 Narrated by Ḥākim Naysābūrī with the above wording; *al-Mustadrak*, vol. II, p. 517. It was also narrated by Tirmidhī in '*Wa-min sūrat wayl li'l-muṭaffifin*,' in *Sunan al-Tirmidhī*, *Kitab Tafsir al-Qur'ān*, no. 3334, with the wording: 'When a slave engages in a contravention, a black spot is dotted on his heart. If he desists, asks forgiveness...' Tirmidhī stated that this saying was well authenticated/rigorously authenticated. Ibn Māja also narrated a report that is close in wording to this one in his *Sunan*.

heart will be touched by rust that may imply unbelief. We seek refuge in God from this! He should not desist from repenting [out of] agreement with the folly of the ego, which may tell him, 'The soul might repent from this sin but you will return to it.' In which case his response should be, 'How do you know that death will not come to me before I return to it so [that] I die repenting of that sin?' Furthermore, the servant should not desist from repenting out of despair of it being accepted, for it has been mentioned in the explanation of the words of God Most High, *And cast not yourselves by your own hands into destruction* (Q.II.195), that this is for the servant who commits great sins and then says to himself, 'I am doomed; no good deed will ever benefit me!' That is to say, do not [allow] yourselves to fall into destruction, [either] through committing great [sins] or by despairing after committing [those sins], and then claiming that [good] deeds never benefitted you in the first place. This is because despair (*ya's*) prevents repentance (*tawba*) and entails destruction. The servant should therefore beware of it.

The servant should also know that when he fears God's vengeance for desisting from repentance, hoping for His forgiveness through the act of repentance and remaining upright in this, he has realised the reality of sincere repentance. Hope (*rajā'*) and fear (*khawf*) also become spiritual stations for him.

THE MANNER OF THE DERIVATION OF MOTIVATING THOUGHTS

You should also know that amongst these four different motivating thoughts only the Angel's inspiration (*lammat al-malak*) and Satan's whispering (*lammat al-shayṭān*) were reported as having been mentioned by the Prophet (may God bless him and grant him peace). It follows from this that the heart is only the battlefield of their armies. It is for this reason that one Sufi master (may God have mercy on him) said, 'The Angel's inspiration and Satan's whispering are the trunk (*aṣl*), and the other two motivating thoughts are a branch (*farʿ*) from the two of them.' This is because when the Angel's inspiration moves the spirit to project a righteous resolve in the heart, and the latter is stirred by this righteous resolve towards the presence of proximity, the beginning of this proximity makes him receive motivating thoughts from the Abidingly Real. On the other hand, when Satan's whispering is moved, the ego plunges into the centre of its instinct (*gharīza*) and innate nature (*ṭab*ʿ) by its own disposition, and, through this movement, it receives motivating thoughts appropriate to its instinct, its innate nature and base desire, such that it insists on them and wilfully persists in seeking them.

However, when the spiritual wayfarer becomes realised through the [station of] extinction (*fanā'*), all motivating thoughts, including the Lordly ones, are negated from him. This is because motivating thoughts are couriers (*rusul*), and sending something with the utmost proximity is not right. The servant in the station of extinction is divested of all created traces (*al-āthār al-muḥdatha*) and is immersed in the sea of Divine Lights (*baḥr al-Anwār al-Ilāhiyya*), of which thoughts cannot conceive. Nonetheless, the servant can be brought back (as far as his servanthood is concerned) from the station of extinction (*maqām al-fanā'*) to the station of subsistence (*maqām al-baqā'*), wherein the Abidingly Real is not veiled from created beings, nor created beings from the Abidingly Real, since they do not change [in the same way that they do] before extinction. At that point, the servant's special existence is bestowed upon him through it, which was the target of the different types of thoughts that cleanses [him] of the blameworthy qualities that he possessed before extinction. He is then characterised by praiseworthy, godly qualities and his existence is illuminated by the Light of the Abidingly Real without the total alterity imagined before extinction. Thus, insofar as his special existence is concerned, the exigencies of the ego, and its thoughts demanding its due rights, return to him. At that juncture, [the ego] deserves to be treated with gentleness by granting it those rights, which, were it to be denied them, would cause an imbalance in its actions due the imbalance of its mind and faculties, thereby unbalancing the whole affair.

The motivating thoughts from the Abidingly Real and those from an Angel also return to the servant, but the motivating thoughts of the ego demanding shares of pleasures do not return to him. So, were any of these thoughts to return, he would not pursue them; for no matter what it may achieve, the ego still contains an element of ignorance that prevents it from distinguishing between what benefits it and what harms it. It is like a child who is allowed to engage in what benefits him and is forbidden from approaching what harms him. At this juncture, he is only treating the soul and the heart with fairness: the heart giving the soul that which it deserves, and the soul giving the heart its due by following in obedience to God Most High. Moreover, the motivating thoughts from Satan will not return to him at this stage. It is to this that God Most High alludes with His words, *Over My servants thou shalt have no authority* (Q.xv.42). As for the Prophetic saying that we mentioned above, it was the one narrated by ʿAbd Allāh b. Masʿūd (may God be well pleased with him) in which the Prophet (may God bless him and grant him peace) said:

> Satan has [an evil] whisper for the son of Adam and the Angel has an inspiration. As for the whispering of Satan, it incites one to evil and to disbelief in the truth. The inspiration of the Angel, on the other hand, prompts one to goodness and to belief in the truth. Whoever experiences the latter, let him know that it is from God (glorified and exalted is He) and praise God. And whoever experiences the former, let him seek refuge in God from Satan the accursed.[1]

1 Narrated by Tirmidhī in '*Wa-min sūrat al-baqara*,' in *Sunan al-Tirmidhī*, *Kitab Tafsir al-Qur'ān*, no. 2988. He stated that this Prophetic saying was well authenticated/isolated (*ḥasan/gharīb*).

Then he recited, *Satan promises you poverty and bids you unto indecency* (Q.II.268). This is because the actions of human beings are subject to their wills, and their wills are subject to their belief [firstly] in benefit through seeking, and [secondly in] harm through fleeing. [This] belief may be correct in that what was believed to be beneficial is indeed beneficial to one's religion and worldly matters, or to one's religion alone; the same applies to that which is believed to be harmful. Or, this belief may be incorrect.

Human capability (*al-quwwa al-bashariyya*) is not sufficient to distinguish genuine benefit from genuine harm, or other things. It is necessary to have an extraneous power (*al-quwwa al-khārijiyya*): either angelic (*malakiyya*), to show humans things as they are in themselves, or demonic (*shayṭāniyya*), to obfuscate matters for them. We say that human capability is not sufficient for doing so because man's perception by means of the five senses (*idrākahu bi'l-ḥawāss*) is confined to apparent matters, while by means of reason (*bi'l-ʿaql*) he is never free from certain [a priori] conceptions as long as reason has not been divested of tenebrous attachments through the support of the light of insight (*bi-nūr al-baṣīra*), in conformity with that which is attested by spiritual experience. For there must necessarily be an extraneous human capability that is similar to Satan inasmuch as he is created from fire, and which is inherent in man's creation inasmuch as he is created from dry clay akin to pottery, for it is understood from this that fire is involved in the creation of man just as fire is involved in the making of pottery.

THE EFFECT OF THE ANGEL'S INSPIRATION AND SATAN'S WHISPERING

Likewise, there must be a [point of] similarity (*munāsaba*) with the Angel, and this similarity is related to man's heart or spirit, for both belong to the World of Command. The Prophet (may God bless him and grant him peace) mentioned the effect of the Angel's inspiration and Satan's whispering on moving from the establishment of the effect to the establishment of the cause, which is that Satan's whispering consists of promising evil by Satan frightening one with poverty when being generous, and with missing out on pleasures when abstaining from desired things, and [similarly] with the risk of injury or humiliation when suppressing one's anger, and with hardship and toil when engaging in acts of worship or turning one's back on this world. As for its effect by means of disbelief, it is [accomplished] by denying the Creator, the prophets, the saints and otherworldly matters, which allows one to indulge in unlawful desired things and to vent one's anger.

The whispering of Satan was mentioned before the Angel's inspiration so that man may purify himself from it in order to be certain of the truth of the Angel's inspiration. The Prophet (may God bless him and grant him peace) informed us that the effect of the Angel's inspiration consists of prompting one to goodness, which leads to a balance of the matters of this world and the next, to drawing close to the Lord of all the Worlds, to moulding oneself from His attributes, to exposing oneself to His reward and to fleeing from His punishment by shunning unlawful desire and anger.

He also informed us that the effect of the Angel's inspiration consists of attesting to the truth of the Abidingly Real (glorified and exalted is He), Who rewards this attestation of truth (*taṣdīq*), and attesting to the truth of prophethood (*nubuwwa*), sainthood (*walāya*) and otherworldly matters, and affirming the validity of each one of these matters by means of proofs through reason (*ʿaqliyya*) or through unveiling (*kashfiyya*), and removing any problematic issues concerning these. The Prophet (may God bless him and grant him peace) then said, 'Whoever experiences that angelic motivating thought, let him know that it is from God,' because the Angel is an intermediary between the Lord and the servant in leading him to that which pleases the Lord and to beauteous self-disclosures, and to praise God in order to be thankful for this blessing so that it increases for him and he receives more of it. God

Most High says, *If you are thankful, surely I will increase you* (Q.XIV.7).

And whoever experiences the other [kind of] motivating thought (in other words, the devilish one), let him seek refuge in God from Satan, for he is the dog unleashed from God's side upon on the servant, and he will not be driven away except by seeking refuge in God. This is because, in most cases, human power is incapable of driving him away through disputation. However, one's seeking refuge in God from Satan only avails the servant if he does what God loves, which is to reject the devilish motivating thought when it first occurs to him and shun it completely; not merely by saying, 'I seek refuge in God from Satan.' Indeed, someone who is about to be devoured by a predatory animal or killed by an enemy will not benefit by simply saying, 'I seek refuge in that impenetrable fortress from you,' while remaining pinned to the spot. He should instead swiftly move away from that spot. [So] draw analogous conclusions from this in all of your affairs with Satan, whether motivating thoughts or otherwise.

Then the Prophet (may God bless him and grant him peace) recited the verse as proof of the Angel's inspiration and Satan's whispering, while clarifying that the Angel's inspiration comes from God Most High. One Sufi master (may God have mercy on him) said:

> It is understood from this verse that the devilish [motivating thought] is also from the ego (*min al-nafs*) in some respects. The effects of both the Angel's inspiration and Satan's whispering are also understood from this verse. As for the effect of the whispering of Satan, it consists [firstly] of that which is alluded to in the verse, *Satan promises you poverty* (Q.II.268)—that is, missing out on wealth and desires without receiving any substitutes for them, and so it is an incitement to evil and denying the truth—and [secondly] *and bids you unto indecency* (Q.II.268). In other words, [he

> bids you] to deny the truth (despite the many proofs for it) and to engage in desires and anger in an unlawful manner even though they have a detrimental effect on the life to come and on destroying the matters of this world and the next, if one cares to reflect.
>
> As for the effect of the inspiration of the Angel, it is alluded to in the words of God Most High, *but God promises you His pardon* (Q.II.268); in other words, [He promises you] His protection, because it entails closeness to Him, the concealment of blameworthy character traits, *and His bounty*, by bestowing a reward that is better than that which has been taken away, and also through the bestowal of special, beauteous self-disclosure (*al-tajallī al-khāṣṣ al-jamālī*). It is therefore a promise of goodness and assent in the truth. Such motivating thoughts are angelic because the Angel's inspiration leads to angelic divestment (*li'l-tajarrud al-malakī*), which is closer to Divine Absoluteness and more distant from bodily attachments. It is also understood from the above Qur'ānic verse that, in a way, Satan's whispering [comes] from the ego (*nafs*) because Satan only acts through the intermediary of the ego's base desire and anger. In that case, the servant considers what the ego loves to be genuinely beneficial and what angers it to be genuinely harmful, without paying heed to the consequences of the harm or benefit in question.

This ends his quotation; and God knows the reality of things best.

As for reason (*ʿaql*), it sometimes accompanies egotistic and devilish motivating thoughts in order to distinguish them from angelic and Lordly motivating thoughts, and this affects establishing proof against the servant due to engaging in things via reason; for when there is no reason, punishment and censure are suspended. At other times, reason accompanies motivating thoughts emanating from the Abidingly Real or an Angel, so that the servant engages in action [both] willingly, and in compliance with God's command; so this provides him with God's good pleasure and reward.

SUMMONING GOOD MOTIVATING THOUGHTS AND WARDING OFF THEIR OPPOSITES

One of the gnostics mentioned that one of the things that encourages the effusion of divine and angelic motivating thoughts is reciting *Sūrat* [*Ikhlāṣ*], *Say, 'He is God, One'* (Q.CXII.1); whereas reciting *Sūrat* [*al-Kāfirūn*], *Say, 'O unbelievers'* (Q.CIX.1), helps to stop egotistic and devilish motivating thoughts.

A NOTE RELATING TO THIS SHORT COMMENTARY. Keep in mind, O desirous student, that whenever we mention the spirit (*rūḥ*) in this short commentary of ours, we mean the spirit from the World of Command (*ʿālam al-amr*), not the animal spirit (*al-rūḥ al-ḥayawānī*) that is from the World of Creation (*ʿālam al-khalq*), which we call 'the soul' (*nafs*) in this short commentary. This animal spirit is found in all animals, for it is the source of the faculties of perception, such as hearing, sight, smell, taste and touch, which are found in all animals, and so their source is found in them also. This spirit is made of an earthly, subtle vapour, which is because it is from a nutriment whose origin is dust. It emanates from the [physical] heart that is known to the common people. This animal spirit is diffused in the path of the cavities of the veins and arteries travelling throughout the whole body.

Due to its being [made] of nutriments, this animal spirit is freely used by the science of medicine on the basis of the indication of its movement (as reflected in the heart's pulse), which shows the balance or imbalance of the temperaments of the four humours. This animal spirit is also found in the foetus while it is like a lump of flesh (*muḍgha*) after preparing the means of its free disposal in the body, and after acquiring its fleshy heart and veins. Then God creates bones from this morsel of flesh and then covers the bones with flesh, after which He breathes the spirit that is specifically assigned to human beings (*al-rūḥ alladhī yukhtaṣṣu bi'l-insān*) into it.

WHAT IS MEANT BY THE HEART?

Likewise, when we mention 'the heart' (*qalb*) in this short commentary, what we mean by it is the human subtlety (*al-laṭīfa al-insāniyya*) that belongs to the World of Command, the rational soul (*al-nafs al- nāṭiqa*), according to the ancient philosophers (*ḥukamā'*), not the heart known by the common people, which is the well-known, pine cone-shaped piece of flesh placed on the left side of the body that is under the left breast by a distance of about two fingers.

The fact that the Prophet (may God bless him and grant him peace) identified this lump of flesh with the heart as related in the Prophetic saying, 'There is a lump of flesh (*muḍgha*) in the body of the son of Adam; when it is good, the whole body is good, and when it is corrupt, the whole body is corrupt. Verily, it is the heart (*qalb*)',[1] was nothing but a way of exaggerating, and he attached the body's goodness or corruption to the goodness or corruption of [this lump of flesh]. So whatever happens to this lump of flesh is what [also] happens to the real heart (*li'l-qalb al-ḥaqīqī*), even if it is only by way of deputyship and substitution, because that human subtlety has a certain connection and special attachment to this lump of flesh. The

1 Narrated by Muḥammad b. Ismāʿīl al-Bukhārī, '*Bāb faḍl man istabra'a li-dīnihi,*' in *Ṣaḥīḥ al-Bukhārī bi-hāshiyat al-Imām al-Sindī, Kitab al-Iman*, Mecca: Maktabat ʿAbbās Aḥmad al-Bāz, [no date], no. 52 and by Muslim, '*Bāb akhdh al-ḥalāl wa-tark al-shubuhāt,*' in *Ṣaḥīḥ Muslim, Kitāb al-musaqāt*, ed. Muḥammad Fu'ād ʿAbd al-Bāqī, Cairo: Dār Iḥyā' al-Kutub al-ʿArabiyya, 1955, no. 1599.

latter is like its nest, habitation or dwelling, and there is a kind of union between them, as if there were no distinction between the two of them.

The two of them may also share some judgements (*baʿḍ al-aḥkām*), and movement in the lump of flesh may appear to be from the remembering of the real heart; and it is to this real heart that God Most High refers in His saying, *Surely in that there is a reminder to him who has a heart* (Q.L.37). And were what is meant [here] by 'the heart' to be the pine cone-shaped piece of flesh, then that would exist in all—even the beasts and the dead.

THE DIFFERENCE BETWEEN HUMAN AND ANIMAL SPIRITS

As for the aforementioned animal spirit, even though it is originally universal, when the Spirit of Sublime Command (*al-Rūḥ al-Amr al-ʿUlwī*) comes upon it, it becomes different from the category of spirits found in all animals. The reason for this is that it acquires another quality of perfect evenness and balanced temperament from the Spirit of Sublime Command that makes it extremely subtle and likened to the heart, which is the rational soul. Hence it becomes a soul (*nafs*) that is a locus for intellection (*maḥall li'l-nuṭq*); in other words, it is a locus for the faculty of thought (*al-quwwa al-mufakkira*) that is attached to the faculty of reasoning (*al-quwwa al-ʿāqila*), which is a faculty of the heart.

It also becomes a locus for inspiration (*li'l-ilhām*)—in other words, through the projection of meanings by means other than the five senses—to the point where it becomes a locus for the divine oath [mentioned] in the saying of God Most High, *By the soul, and That which shaped it* (Q.XCI.7). Here, God Most High swore by the animal spirit when it acquires evenness through a balanced temperament. [The animal spirit acquires this evenness] because it becomes a soul (*nafs^an*) that is receptive to the inspiration of debauchery (*fujūr*) and God-fearingness (*taqwā*), which are both a locus of manifestation for His Rigour and His Beauty, respectively. And both [debauchery and God-fearingness] inspire [the animal spirit by] extending their invitation [to it]. The evenness (*taswiya*) of the animal spirit therefore happens when the Spirit of Sublime Command comes upon it, for before that it was far from being even, just like the spirits of all other animals.

At the arrival of the Spirit upon it, it acquires a balanced evenness that separates it from the category of animal spirits and, thus, it becomes so receptive to the self-disclosure (*li-tajallī*) of both majesty (*jalāl*) and beauty (*jamāl*) that its Creator swears by it as though He swears by His Own Essence, due to the similarity between the loci of manifestation and He Who manifests those loci.

THE IMPORTANCE PAID TO THE SOUL BY THE PROPHET

Abū Hilal (may God be well pleased with him and benefit by him) related that whenever the Messenger of God (may God bless him and grant him peace) recited the verse, *Prosperous is he who purifies it* (Q.XCI.9), he would stop his recitation and then say, 'O God! Grant my soul its God-fearingness. You are its Guardian and Master! Purify it; You are the best Who can purify it.'[1] Despite the perfection of his state (may God bless him and grant him peace), he placed great importance on the matter of the soul because he knew that prosperity depends on its purification. He also knew that its purification could not happen by means of his own self, but [only] by means of his Lord through the emanation of God-fearingness upon him (*bi-ifāḍat al-taqwā ʿalayhi*). This is why he said, 'O God! Grant my soul its God-fearingness'; in other words, that which saves it from fatal sins and deficiencies. And then he said, 'I am as weak as a small child in this, "You are its Guardian"; in fact, I am completely incapable of purifying it by myself for I am a slave and You are its Master.' Then he said after it had acquired the quality of God-fearingness, 'Purify it from its own self, as well as from

1 Narrated by Muslim, *Ṣaḥīḥ Muslim, Kitāb al-dhikr wa'l-duʿā' wa'l-tawba wa'l-istighfār*, no. 2722.

anything other than You, through You. You are indeed the Best One Who can purify it.'

Because of this, the animal spirit is not sublime (as has already been mentioned). In most cases, its sustenance lies in the application of God's *Sunna* through food. We say 'in most cases' because God is capable of giving it strength without food, as happens in rare situations when foods are not digested due to sickness or other factors.

THE REASONS FOR NOT BEING HARMED BY HUNGER OR LACK OF SLEEP

An example of this is what happens to some people who can abstain from food for forty days or so without feeling hungry or being harmed by hunger. This happens for one of two reasons: (1) either the light of self-disclosure (*nūr al-tajallī*) so overwhelms one that it prevents the soul (*nafs*) from managing the affairs of the body (*badan*) by breaking down food substances and feeding the whole body, as is the case with a sick person; or (2) [it is because of] joy in one's Lord (*al-faraḥ bi-Rabbihi*) as its coolness quells hunger. In [this state of] joy, coolness conquers heat; whereas in [a state of] fear (*khawf*), one of the two heats conquers the other. This is an observed fact, as in the case of a person who no longer feels hungry when joy visits him, and the same is observed when fear overwhelms a person.

Similarly, [the Sufis] say, 'Staying awake at night because of intimacy (*uns*) does not harm one. This is because the nature of sleep (*ṭabᶜ al-nawm*) is cold and humid and the nature of intimacy (*ṭabᶜ al-uns*) is also cold and humid; so when one of them is absent while the other is present, it stands in its place. This is the reason why the Gnostics who know their state of intimacy with the Genuine Beloved (*al-Maḥbūb al-Ḥaqīqī*) are not harmed by staying awake at night.'

You should also know that this joy in God Most High only happens to the one who sincerely abstains from food for God, pure from any blemish of base desire in [his] soul. When this is the case,

God grants him instead such joy in his inward aspect (*fī bāṭinihi*) that it makes him forget food and drink, because this joy is the result of a [kind of] pleasure [that is] strong and genuine; whereas the pleasure of food is only the result of a weak desire.

As for the person who abstains from food without sincerity (*min ghayr al-ikhlāṣ*), he is far from experiencing such joy. God only bestows such joy upon the sincere person because he is free of the obstacles that bar him from the way of the Abidingly Real (*ṭarīq al-Ḥaqq*). He therefore encounters the Beloved without any veil (*bi-lā ḥijāb*), so exhilaration overwhelms him to the extent that he forgets hunger, food and drink. And [it may be that] he does not completely forget food or drink, but when his heart is filled with the lights of He Who disclosed Himself to his spirit (*bi-anwār man tajallā li-rūḥihi*), he is pulled into the World of the Transcendent Spirit (*ʿĀlam al-Rūḥ al-Rūḥānī*) after wavering between the spirit and the soul due to the powerful pull of the Transcendent Spirit, until he is pulled to the original centre (*al-markaz al-aṣlī*) situated in the Spiritual World (*al-ʿĀlam al-Rūḥānī*), which is of the World of the Higher Intellects (*ʿĀlam al-ʿUqūl al-ʿĀliya*).

THE REFLECTION OF THE LIGHTS OF THE SPIRIT ON THE HEART AND SOUL

By means of this pull, the person transcends the region of egotistic desires (*al-shahwa al-nafsāniyya*), as if they exercise no attraction at all due to the weakness of their attraction, thanks to the tranquillity of the soul (*li-ṭuma'nīnat al-nafs*) and the reflection of the lights of the spirit on it (*inʿikās anwār al-rūḥ ʿalayhā*) through the intermediary of the heart, which, in one respect, is illumined by the light of the spirit and which, in another, itself illumines the soul. Thus, whenever the heart has been pulled towards the abyss of the spirit, the peaceful soul follows it; so it corresponds to the heart. Whenever the soul corresponds to the heart by means of the reflection of the light of the spirit, which reaches it through the heart, at that point a spirit comes to be in the soul (*yaṣīru fī al-nafs rūḥ*[un])—in other words, a spiritual light (*nūr rūḥānī*), which is almost like the spirit, just as the fiery heat in wood that is adjacent to a fire becomes almost like fire.

The heart (*qalb*) has taken this state from the spirit (*rūḥ*) insofar as it has free disposal, and it delivers it to the soul (*nafs*) insofar as it is attached to it, so the soul becomes like the heart, [and] even like the spirit. So the spirit pulls the soul through the intermediary of the resulting correspondence between them due to the effect of the spiritual light that is in the soul, which leads to it being overwhelmed by spirituality (*rūḥāniyya*). At this point it is also pulled towards the World of the Spirits (*ʿĀlam al-Arwāḥ*), and takes pleasure in genuine higher joys, and looks down on worldly foods because they are lowly bestial desires that are common to all animals. This is indeed a noble pleasure in which freely disposed spirits (*al-arwāḥ al-mujarrada*) partake amongst the Archangels (*al-Malā'ika al-Muqarrabīn*).

Only then will the person who possesses this state be realised in accordance with the meaning of the saying of the Prophet (God bless him and grant him peace), 'I spend the night with my Lord Who feeds me and gives me to drink.'[1] In other words, my soul dwells in the spiritual station (*al-maqām al-rūḥānī*) near the Divine Presence (*al-Ḥaḍra al-Ilāhiyya*), which feeds me the pleasures of Its Self-Disclosures and gives me Its Love to drink, and these become substitutes for physical food and drink, which are so despicable in comparison. The Prophet (may God bless him and grant him peace) said this when he was asked about his fasting for days and nights without a break, even though he forbade those who were not fit for that from doing so, lest their physical vehicles be weakened, thereby [causing them to] also miss the actual acts of worship.

No one is able to withstand continuous fasting as just described

1 Narrated by Bukhārī, '*Bāb al-iqtidā' bi-afʿāl al-nabī*,' in *Ṣaḥīḥ al-Bukhārī*, *Kitāb al-iʿtiṣām bi'l-Kitāb wa'l-Sunna*, no. 72980 and by Muslim, '*Bāb al-nahy ʿan al-wiṣāl fī al-ṣawm*,' in *Ṣaḥīḥ Muslim*, *Kitāb al-ṣiyām*, no. 1103.

except a servant whose actions (other than acts of worship) and whose speech (other than reciting the Qur'ān, glorifying God, seeking forgiveness from Him or any of his states relating to the Afterlife) become necessary. This is because this accustoms the soul to necessities so that it only partakes of food when necessary; otherwise, the soul will manifest its tyranny. When the soul manifests its tyranny in one thing, it fails to show temperance in other things. Thus, if the servant were to utter a single word unnecessarily, the fire of hunger would burn him just as fire easily burns alfalfa when it is dry. This is because the dormant soul (*al-nafs al-rāqida*)—in other words, the soul which, through spiritual discipline (*riyāḍa*), has become close to voluntary death, which is spiritual extinction (*fanā'*), but is not completely dead—awakens due to indiscreetness and to engaging in excesses. When it awakens, it engages in all its requisites, for when excesses creep in, the soul inclines towards its base desire.

Now, if one knew that holding fast to necessities (*ḍarūrāt*) and shunning all excesses (*fuḍūliyyāt*) were a condition of the ability to fast continuously, then the servant who is meant for this would find it easy to fast continuously, if he understood how to direct his soul in such a way that necessities were distinct from excesses to him. When he is granted perfect knowledge of the distinction between necessities and excesses, and does not cease this habit and state of his with his soul, he will receive assistance from God Most High by [His] granting him a joy that will make him forget food and drink.

Joy will especially overwhelm him when divine gifts are revealed to him in recompense for foregoing food. This is like presenting a person with an apple when his hunger has reached its utmost, only for him to see a fair maiden of Paradise in the middle of the apple as a recompense for his patience when breaking it to eat it; and so this person becomes so happy with what he sees that he forgoes food for a few more days. The fact that a fair maiden of Paradise was made to appear to this person from the apple is a miracle (*karāma*) within a miracle, and the World of Divine Power (*ʿĀlam al-Qudra*) has been revealed to him along with the World of Causality (*ʿĀlam al-Ḥikma*).

FAITH IN DIVINE POWER

Faith in Divine Power (*al-īmān bi'l-Qudra*) is one of the pillars of faith in God because it is faith in the Essence of God Most High and all His Attributes with which He has described Himself in His Book and upon the tongues of His prophets (blessings and peace be upon them). The inclusion of something of great measure in something small is associated with Divine Power because the 'measure' (*miqdār*) [of a thing] is amongst its accidents (*ʿawāriḍ*); it is therefore possible that that which is being included (*dākhil*) [in something] may clothe itself in some small measure immediately upon its inclusion (*ḥāla dukhūlihi*) [in it]; so whenever it emerges [from it], it has been clothed in great measure despite its duration and original form remaining unchanged. Therefore, accept this statement on account of its possibility, and do not deny [it] because of its mere improbability.

THE SECRET OF THE POWER OF CONTINUAL FASTING

Through what we have mentioned above, one may understand the secret (*sirr*) behind many Friends of God (*awliyā' Allāh*) who have abstained from food, drink and sleeping for a long period of time, as was the case with the Prophetic descendant, the Pole Shaykh al-Muqaddam Muḥammad b. ʿAlī ʿAlawī [1] (may God benefit by him), who spent 100 days [that is, 100 days and nights] without tasting

1 The Imam, the Foremost Jurisprudent (*al-Faqīh al-Muqaddam*), Muḥammad b. ʿAlī b. Muḥammad b. ʿAlawī al-Ḥusaynī al-Ḥaḍramī, the resident of Mirbāṭ and the uncontested master of the ʿAlawī group (*ṭā'ifa*), who was called the Greatest Master (*al-Ustādh al-Aʿẓam*). He was born in Tarim in the year 574/1178, memorised the Qur'ān while still a boy and then pursued sacred knowledge with traditional scholars. He has written several epistles including *Badā'iʿ ʿulūm al-mukāshafāt wa'l-tajalliyāt*. He died in Tarim in 653/1255. See Shillī, *al-Mashraʿ al-rawī*, vol. II, pp. 2–11; Ḥabshī, *ʿIqd al-yawāqīt*, vol. II, pp. 126–127; and Ziriklī, *al-Aʿlām*, vol. VI, p. 282.

food or water. This was also the case with the Pole, the Prophetic descendant al-Sayyid ʿUmar al-Miḥḍār ʿAlawī (may God benefit by him), who fasted continuously for 40 days, and then added another 40 days of continuous fasting from food and water to it when he travelled on foot to [perform] the Pilgrimage. During this period, his strength was never affected and he was never too weak to walk. He also spent five years not consuming any of the foods that human beings usually eat, and one month in which he only drank water, without being affected in the slightest by this. This was also the case with the Pole, the Prophetic descendant Shaykh ʿAbd Allāh al-ʿAydarūs ʿAlawī (may God benefit by him), who fasted for a number of years, only breaking his fast [by eating] seven dates. This was also the case with the Pole Saʿd b. ʿAli,[1] the companion of ʿAydarūs (may God benefit by both of them), who used to fast continuously for 40 days, only breaking his fast with water. And this was also the case with the Prophetic descendant Shaykh Aḥmad Bājaḥdab ʿAlawī[2] (may God benefit by him), who did not taste anything but coffee in the last three years of his life. This is as far as food and drink are concerned.

1 The Imam, Shaykh Saʿd b. ʿAlī b. ʿAbd Allāh Bāmadhaj al-Ḥaḍramī al-Tarīmī, better known as al-Suwaynī. He began his learning with the memorisation and study of the Qur'ān and later studied *fiqh*. He was known for his many retreats. He never married and died in 857/1453. See ʿAbd al-Qādir b. Shaykh b. ʿAbd Allāh al-ʿAydarūs, *al-Nūr al-sāfir ʿan akhbār al-qarn al-ʿāshir*, ed. Aḥmad Ḥālū et al., Beirut: Dār Ṣādir, 2001, pp. 595–605.

2 The Imam, Aḥmad b. ʿAlawī b. al-Muʿallam b. Muḥammad b. ʿAlī Jaḥdab b. ʿAbd al-Raḥmān b. Muḥammad b. al-Shaykh ʿAbd Allāh Bā ʿAlawī, who was known by the name of his grandfather, Jaḥdab, was born in Tarim and studied under the greatest men of the city. He used to be counted amongst the men of *The Treatise of Qushayrī* (al-Risāla al-Qushayriyya) on account of the intensity of his scrupulousness (*waraʿihi*), his mortification of the flesh (*taqashshufihi*) and the uprightness of his Sufi order (*wa-istiqāmat ṭarīqatihi*), and he transmitted traditions about renunciation from the world. He died in Tarim in the year 973/1565. See Shillī, *al-Mashraʿ al-rawī*, vol. II, pp. 70–73; ʿAydarūs, *al-Nūr al-sāfir*, p. 385; and ʿAbd al-Ḥayy b. Aḥmad Abū al-Falāḥ b. al-ʿImād, *Shadharāt al-dhahab fī akhbār man dhahab*, ed. ʿAlī Mahmud al-Arna'ūt, Damascus: Dār Ibn Kathīr, 1986–1995 vol. x, p. 541.

As for sleeping, an example of this is what happened to the Pole, the Prophetic descendant Shaykh ʿAbd al-Raḥmān al-Saqqāf ʿAlawī[1] (may God benefit by him), who did not sleep for 35 years. Likewise, his grandson, Shaykh ʿAbd Allāh al-ʿAydarūs, did not sleep during the day or at night for more than ten years. Saʿd b. ʿAli, the companion of ʿAydarūs who was mentioned above, also did not sleep during the day or at night for a number of years. Similarly, the son of ʿAydarūs, the Pole Shaykh Abū Bakr (may God benefit by him), did not sleep more than three hours a day over a period of 30 years. The same happened to numerous friends of God Most High, and whoever consults the sources will find their stories there.

A NOTE CONCERNING CONTINUAL FASTING. One should also know that if it were the case that continuous fasting or reducing one's intake of food and sleep were the very epitome of virtue, then none of the prophets (may God bless them and grant them peace) would have neglected them, and the Messenger of God (may God bless him and grant him peace) would have reached the extreme limit of it. Undoubtedly, there is undeniable merit in the above; however, God's gifts are not bound by this. There might be someone who eats every day who is better than someone who fasts continuously for 40 days, just as there might be someone to whom none of the miraculous disclosures of God's Divine Power are revealed, but who is better than someone to whom these are revealed when God reveals them to him through pure gnosis (*bi-ṣirf al-maʿrifa*). The [revealing of His] Divine Power is a vestige of the station (*maqām*), and whoever is made fit to be near the All-Powerful (*Qādir*) is not

1 The Imam ʿAbd al-Raḥmān b. Muḥammad Mawlā al-Duwayla b. ʿAlī b. ʿAlawī b. al-Faqīh al-Muqaddam. He was better known by the name 'al-Saqqāf,' because he towered (*saqafa*) over the saints of his time. He was born in Tarim in the year 739/1338. He memorised the Qur'ān and mastered the different readings and recitations of the Qur'ān. He also travelled in pursuit of sacred knowledge. He died in the year 819/1416 and was buried in the Zanbal cemetery in Tarim. See Shillī, *al-Mashraʿ al-rawī*, vol. II, pp. 141–146 and Ḥabshī, *ʿIqd al-yawāqīt*, vol. II, pp. 121–122.

amazed by Divine Power, nor does he deem anything from it to be too much. Rather, he sees that Divine Power is disclosed to him from the inward parts of the World of Causality (*ʿĀlam al-Ḥikma*). So understand!

Now, even though we have somehow deliberated a great deal on the animal spirit (which is the soul) and the heart (which is the rational soul according to the ancient philosophers) in this short commentary, we would like to mention here what our master and grandfather, the Pole, the Master, Shaykh b. ʿAbd Allāh al-ʿAydarūs[1] (may God benefit by them), said regarding the human spirit in his book, *The Verities of Divine Oneness and the Heart-Softenings of Isolation* (Ḥaqā'iq al-tawḥīd wa-raqā'iq al-tafrīd).[2]

THE HUMAN SPIRIT

This is what he wrote:

> You should know that God Most High created the human spirit (*al-rūḥ al-insāniyya*) from the Light of His Essence and deposited all divine knowledges (*jamīʿ al-ʿulūm al-ilāhiyya*) in it through the intermediary of the intellect (*ʿaql*). It is therefore inherently predisposed to directly apprehend verities through its primordial nature (*bi'l-fiṭra*). That which has

1 The prophetic descendant, Imam, Shaykh and Knower of God, Shaykh b. ʿAbd Allāh b. Shaykh b. al-Shaykh ʿAbd Allāh al-ʿAydarūs, was born in Tarim in the year 919/1513 and grew up there. He travelled to India in the year 958/1551 and stayed there for around 32 years. He left a number of works to posterity, including *The Prophetic Necklace and the Muṣṭafan Secret* (al-ʿIqd al-nabawī wa'l-sirr al-muṣṭafawī), *The Triumph and the Glad Tidings* (al-Fawz wa'l-bushrā) and others. He died in India in the year 990/1582 in the city of Ahmedabad. See Shillī, *al-Mashraʿ al-rawī*, vol. II, pp. 119–122; ʿAydarūs, *al-Nūr al-sāfir*, pp. 488–495; and Ibn al-ʿImād, *Shadharāt al-dhahab*, p. 620.

2 This is his major commentary on his poem about the tenets of faith entitled, *Tuḥfat al-murīd*. He has another minor commentary entitled, *Sirāj al-tawḥīd*. See ʿAydarūs, *al-Nūr al-sāfir*, p. 492.

veiled people from such an apprehension is the power of the body with which the spirit is intermingled, and due to this intermingling, the spirit has become low and abased. When the servant engages in spiritual discipline, the veils are lifted, because the body loosens its grip on the spirit when the servant reduces his intake of food, and minimises his talking, his sleeping and mixing with other people.

If to this one adds abstention from such habits as anxiety, surrendering to one's thoughts and looking out for people in them, or being happy with what comes to one and sad because of what is out of reach, and similar habits, then the spirit frees itself from the prison of inherent nature and flies in the sky of the World of Spirits. And if, in addition to all of this, the servant abandons analogical thinking (*al-qiyās bi'l-ʿaql*) in his pursuit of the knowledge (*maʿrifa*) of things, then things will appear to him as they are in themselves: neither veiled by walls nor made inaccessible by the remoteness of time or place. Things may even be seen with the physical eye due to the union of the light of the heart with the eye. In this case, it is admissible to call the heart of such a servant (*qalbuhu*) 'the Preserved Tablet' (*al-Lawḥ al-Maḥfūẓ*), and his spirit 'the Mother of the Book' (*Umm al-Kitāb*).

ANOTHER NOTE CONCERNING THE TERM, 'SECRET'. One of the Gnostics (may God benefit by him) said:

As for the term, 'the secret' (*sirr*), it is—and

God knows best—an allusion to something that is not independent of quiddity (*māhiyya*); so it is not something that has a separate definition. This is why the Folk (*Qawm*) have alluded to it in a manner that does not fully define it, and not in terms of a particular description of one thing [literally, 'matter']. For this reason, there is some disagreement about it. This disagreement cannot be reconciled if one accepts that it is a description of one specific thing, since some of them have placed it above the heart (*fawq al-qalb*) and below the spirit (*dūn al-rūḥ*); while above the spirit (*fawq al-rūḥ*), they have placed what they termed, 'the hidden' (*khafī*).

Some of them, however, have placed [the secret] above the spirit—meaning that it is subtler than the spirit. Their proof that the secret is above the spirit is that the secret is the locus of witnessing (*mushāhada*) until the point when it is annihilated and becomes the hidden. The spirit, on the other hand, is the locus of love (*maḥabba*) which is before witnessing, as witnessing is only the certitude that results from the predominance of love. The heart, in turn, is the locus of gnosis (*maʿrifa*), which is one of the causes of love. It is the locus of gnosis because it has one side facing the spirit and one side facing the soul, and both the spirit and the soul [have the ability to] perceive (*mudrikān*): the spirit perceives intelligible matters, while the soul perceives sensory matters.

PROOF THAT THE SECRET IS NOT INDEPENDENT

OF QUIDDITY. The proof that the secret is not independent of quiddity is that, if it were truly independent, it would have been mentioned in the Sufis' earlier treatises or as part of their nomenclature, since this is a tremendous matter. However, only the spirit and heart are mentioned in spite of the fact that other things lower than it have also been mentioned.

Likewise, proof that it is not a particular description comes from the disagreement about it amongst the People of Unveiling (*Ahl al-Kashf*), a disagreement which cannot be reconciled if one were to accept that it is a description relating to one specific thing. This is in spite of the fact that they are People of Unveiling, and unveiling precludes absolute error from happening in it. This is why they have not completely rejected the unveiling of anyone amongst them. Rather, they interpret each unveiling in a correct way that befits the Divine Presence, even when the interpretation is only remotely plausible.

Yes, it is true that solely restricting the authenticity and correctness of something to one's personal spiritual experience is rejected; however, on the whole, no one does this except for someone who is overwhelmed by spiritual drunkenness. And when this is the case, then we say (and God knows best) that what is called 'the secret' is not an independent thing in itself. What we mean by 'independent' (*mustaqill*) here is that it does not have an existence (*wujūd*) or quiddity (*māhiyya*) that are not subordinate to something else; unlike the spirit and the soul which have existences and quiddities that are not subordinate to anything else.

The secret is only the heart (*qalb*), which is described by the quality of the spirit, and the spirit (*rūḥ*), which is described by the quality of the Divine Essence. However, because this description is so subtle, it almost turns what it describes into something else—to the point where those who experience it find it to be unintelligible, which leads them to think it is a subdivision (*qism*) that has an independent existence and essence. This is because when it is cleansed of animal turbidity and purified of its tenebrous qualities, the spirit breaks free from the shackles of the darkness of the soul and ascends to the abodes of proximity that correspond to it by dint of its original creation, from which it was kept away due to the shackles of the soul's darkness.

At this point, the heart follows the spirit and shifts from its dwelling abode, which is equidistant between the spirit and the soul, and it longs to acquire the qualities of the spirit in terms of purity (*ṣafā'*) and divestment (*tajarrud*) through which ascent to the stations of proximity takes place. And so, in divestment it acquires an added quality in addition to the qualities of which it is already possessed; and this obscures it for those who experience it due to this added quality, which, up to that point, was never one of the qualities of the heart. And because they saw that it was purer than the heart, they called it 'the secret;' but it is none other than the heart itself with the added quality of purity.

Thus, when the heart has acquired a quality in addition to those [that it already possessess] by ascending to the spirit, the spirit has also acquired an additional quality of purity and divestment, which help with its ascent insofar as it has rid the darkness from the undutiful heart's disposal (*tadbīr*), which turns the heart, in this case, into a dutiful heart. This quality has appeared as being unintelligible to those who have experienced it amongst the People of Unveiling, but they have also called it 'the secret.' And so 'the secret' (*sirr*) became a term with a common meaning to which have been added the qualities of purity, divestment and ascent.

There is therefore no disagreement between the People of Unveiling about the meaning [of the term], for all of the meanings that they have described can be reconciled, even if they disagree about what they describe. Those who stated that it is subtler than the spirit, mean that it is subtler in quality than the quality of the spirit as perceived by the common people. For it is a spirit characterised by a more particular and subtle quality than what they were acquainted with, even though it is something other than the Universal Spirit (*al-Rūḥ bi'l-Kulliyya*) as one might be led to think judging from their expressions. Thus, that which they have called 'secret' before the spirit is none other than the heart. Nay, it is a heart that has assumed an additional quality to those with which they were usually acquainted. And this ascent (*hādha al-taraqqī*) is not confined to the heart and spirit; rather, in such an ascent, the soul also ascends to the locus of the heart, in the process acquiring the qualities of the heart and shedding its own qualities. However, because of the proximity of its matter, it is not unintelligible to those who have experienced its state, so they know that it is the soul (*nafs*), whose qualities have been substituted by those of the heart.

Peacefulness (*ṭama'nīna*) is amongst its qualities when it follows the spirit, and so it becomes at peace. The sign of its peacefulness is that it becomes an instrument that wants many of the wishes of the heart (*murādāt al-qalb*) before its ascent to the station of the heart. However, we have qualified this wanting of the wishes of the heart before its ascent, because after its ascent, the soul is unable to want all of the aims of the heart as afterwards the heart only wants what its Lord wants, thereby exonerating itself of any power (in other words, of any power to turn away from disobedience): to be able to engage in acts of obedience; to will anything whatsoever; or to choose anything for itself, or for anybody else. In such a scenario, the will of the heart is annihilated (*fāniya*), but the soul can never be thus as long as it remains subsistent (*bāqiya*).

> We have also qualified the wishes of the soul by saying in the above, 'many of the wishes of the heart', because the soul (*nafs*) wants its due in terms of necessary desires, whereas the heart does not want that in and of itself (*bi'l-dhāt*), but only out of gentleness towards the soul, which is attracted to it. Otherwise, the heart has been completely annihilated from its will and has subsisted through the Abidingly Real for it has completely tasted the savour of servanthood (*ṭaʿm al-ʿubūdiyya*), and its servanthood is consecrated to the Abidingly Real due to the fact that it has become free from the slavery of its wants and choices, and the soul shares its servanthood with it, as we have already mentioned.

I say, it is possible to interpret the terms, 'the hidden' (*khafī*) and 'hiddenness' (*ikhfā'*), which are found in the speech of the Sufis (may God benefit by them), along the same lines that the term 'secret' has been interpreted; and God knows the realities of things. It is because of this that it is said that the disagreement concerning some of the statements of the Sufis was only in terms of wording (*lafẓī*) and point of view (*iʿtibārī*). This was the case with Imam Ghazālī (may God benefit by him), who stated that the station of veracity (*ṣiddīqiyya*) was below prophethood (*nubuwwa*), with no intermediary; whereas Imam Muhyī al-Dīn b. al-ʿArabī[1] (may God benefit by him) stated that the station of proximity (*qurba*) was above the station of veracity and below the station of prophethood. This is because proximity is one of the degrees of veracity, and it is the highest of them, just as, for example, *al-Wasīla* is the highest [abode] of Paradise.

It was to this that our teacher, the very learned, the Prophetic

1 See Muḥyī al-Dīn Muḥammad b. ʿAlī b. ʿArabī, *al-Futuḥāt al-makkiyya*, Dār Ṣādir, [no date], vol. II, p. 41.

descendant, the Pole Shaykh ʿAbd Allāh b. Jaʿfar Madhar ʿAlawī[1] (may God benefit by him), alluded regarding ʿAydarūs when he said, 'The Pole of beauty, the possessor of glory and its radiance / Who occupies the station of the peak of proximity.'

On Spiritual Wayfarers and Spiritual Guides

THE FOUR CATEGORIES OF SPIRITUAL WAYFARERS

As for [the Shaykh's] saying in his poetry, 'O spiritual wayfarer' (*yā sālik*), he means wayfarer on the path of the People of Truth. Spiritual wayfarers are divided into four categories: (1) the bare wayfarer (*sālik mujarrad*), who has not progressed to spiritual states due to the hold of deficiency over his spiritual works to the point where they are not a reason for the inclusiveness of spiritual states; (2) the spiritually attracted (*majdhūb*), who has been cut off from spiritual works and not brought back [to them]; (3) the spiritual wayfarer caught by divine attraction (*sālik mutadārik bi'l-jadhba*), but who is brought back to spiritual states; and (4) the spiritually attracted caught by spiritual wayfaring (*majdhūb mutadārik bi'l-sulūk*), but who is brought back to spiritual works.

It is to the last two categories that the words of God Most High alluded to in [the verse], *God chooses unto Himself whomsoever He will, and He guides to Himself whosoever turns, penitent* (Q.XLII.13). That is to say, God chooses unto Himself whomever He wills from amongst His servants, with no prior effort on his part, but rather through His pure, eternal Will that is associated with the perfect readiness of the

1 The master, the Imam ʿAbd Allāh b. Jaʿfar b. ʿAlawī Madhar was born in the city of al-Shaḥar in the year 1093/1682. He travelled to the Hijaz and to India, where he remained for about twenty years. When he left India, he settled in Mecca and lived there until his death in the year 1160/1747. He left a number of books to posterity, including *Kashf al-asrār ʿulūm al-muqarrabīn* and *al-La'āli' al-jawhariyya ʿalā al-ʿaqā'id al-banūfriyya*. See ʿAbd al-Raḥmān b. Ḥasan al-Jabartī, *ʿAjā'ib al-āthār fī al-tarājim wa'l-akhbār aw Ta'rīkh al-Jabartī*, Cairo: al-Maṭbaʿa al-ʿĀmiriyya al-Sharafiyya, 1322/1904, vol. 1, p. 169 and Ismāʿīl b. Muḥammad b. Amīn al-Baghdādī al-Bābānī, *Hadiyyat al-ʿārifīn*, Beirut: Dār al-Fikr, 1982, vol. 1, p. 482.

servant's immutable entities (*ʿaynihi al-thābita*)—which implies the perfection of his balanced temperament, so that the judgements of unity dominate over those of multiplicity, and those of necessity dominate over those of possibility, so that they draw close to God and become attracted to Him through the original love (*al-maḥabba al-aṣliyya*).

As for His words, *and He guides to Himself whosoever turns, penitent*, it means that He chooses unto Himself by making the path of arrival easy for whoever turns [towards God] in penitence and in loyalty to the covenant of repentance due to the deficiency from which the servant's immutable entity may suffer when it does not turn in penitence. When turning [towards God] in penitence (*ināba*) is complete, the path to God Most High becomes easy through His pure favour. Otherwise, mere works do not lead to [that destination]. And even though it is a type of attraction from God Most High, and because it is heavy on their egos, the servants' spiritual struggle (*mujāhada*) becomes a means attributable to them that implies that spiritual states flow onto them. This is because God (glorified and exalted is He) has linked their guidance in the Tablet of Destiny (*fī Lawḥ al-Qadar*) to turning [towards Him] in penitence. The general guidance (*al-hidāya al-ʿāmma*) referred to in the above Qur'ānic verse is the guidance to seek God, while the specific guidance (*al-hidāya al-khāṣṣa*) in this verse refers to guidance towards God; in other words, guidance to unveiling by the lights of His Attributes, Names and Essence.

The spiritual wayfarers who belong to the fourth category are distinguished by pure selection, which is drawing close to God without any prior acquisition [of spiritual works]. Those who belong to the third category are distinguished by guidance on the condition of turning [towards God] in penitence, which is a prior acquisition that yields their spiritual states and stations. Even though it is by God's pure favour, this selection indicates a perfect readiness that draws the emanation of God's favour through the onset of purification. As for pure selection (*al-ijtibāʾ al-maḥḍ*), it is not caused by the servant's acquisition—because acquisition is posterior to it, and that which is posterior cannot be valid as a cause for what is anterior to it—and neither the readiness of the servant's immutable entity, nor his balanced temperament, are of his [own] acquisition; and this is the state of the wayfarers who belong to the fourth category.

SPIRITUAL WAYFARERS WHO ARE QUALIFIED FOR THE OFFICE OF SPIRITUAL GUIDANCE

The first two categories of spiritual wayfarers are not qualified for the office of spiritual guidance (*liʾl-mashayakha*) [that is, guiding others on the spiritual path]. Instead, one should [only] seek their blessings and request their prayers. This is because the spiritual wayfarer who is divested of spiritual states cannot be fit for the office of spiritual guidance, nor will he attain it in the first place due to the lingering remnants of his ego's traits (*ṣifāt nafsihi*). If such a person does not have any spiritual states, how can anybody gain these states from him?

Nay, such a person is at a standstill in his share of God's Mercy and His Given Success to perform righteous works at the station of spiritual dealing and discipline (*maqām al-muʿāmala waʾl-riyāḍa*). He is unable to rise above his rank to a state by which he may dampen the flames of endurance, and so his love is not fulfilled—and this is so as to find joy in his Beloved—so he draws closer to Him until, through Him, he draws closer to Him.

The same applies to the one who is spiritually attracted, who is divested of works. This refers to the one with no wayfaring or spiritual struggle in the desert of the Abidingly Real through the signs of certitude, and from whose heart God has lifted some of the tenebrous veils, so that he finds joy in his Beloved. Even though such a person is perfected in one respect, he is nonetheless unqualified to perfect others as he is not well versed in the path of spiritual dealing (*fī ṭarīq al-muʿāmala*). Spiritual dealing has a complete impact on bringing spiritual wayfarers close to God, but such a person's perfection is lacking as he is at a standstill in his share of closeness to God Most High, finding comfort in his state and without being inclined [to perform any of] his works except those that are obligatory.

As for those who *are* qualified for the office of spiritual guidance, they are restricted to the last two categories of spiritual wayfarers, the first of which relates to the spiritual wayfarer who is caught by divine attraction. At first, he is the lover (*muḥibb*), but in the end, he [becomes] the one who is loved (*maḥbūb*). He is a lover insofar as his first step consists of spiritual struggle and endurance by engaging his body parts in spiritual works, and dealing sincerely and loyally; and also by fulfilling all of the conditions involved in accordance with the endeavours of the heart. In this way, the light flows from the outward (*ẓāhir*) to his inward aspect (*bāṭinihi*), and he becomes loved. His love and joy are therefore completed, and he emerges from the flames of endurance, through works, to the comfort of his spiritual state. He then tastes sweetness after tasting bitterness; enjoys the comfort of the breezes of Divine Favour through the dissipation of the clouds of the ego's traits from him; emerges from the constriction of endurance to the vastness of ease, which happens to his spirit due to cutting off the ego's invitation to base [things] (*sufl*); finds solace in the fragrance of proximity to the extent that he forgets lowly, ephemeral pleasures; and the door of witnessing is opened to him, which is leagues greater than all the lowly pleasures.

At this point, he has found his cure from the disease of inclining to that which is low, and the light of his inward aspect becomes perfected to the extent that his inward vessel flows into his outward aspect, and his outward aspect becomes illumined by the light of his inward aspect. When this happens, he utters words of wisdom that emanate from the perfection of his inward aspect's light, to the point where the hearts of those who listen to him [also] become illumined and lean towards him. The illuminations of the Unseen (*futūḥ al-Ghayb*) then come to him in succession, lights after lights; and his outward aspect becomes rightly guided by spiritual works, and his inward aspect beholds beauty and majesty.

At this juncture, he is fit to be unveiled (*jilwa*) because he is not veiled from anything, by anything. In fact, the spiritual meanings that he acquired during his retreat will stay with him, because he is in a position to dominate and influence all things, while nothing that he sees or hears will have any impact on him. How could this not be so when he is able to seize those who are still imperfect on the spiritual path from their lowlands, and lift them to the rank of perfection? But he is not seized by his ego, by Satan, or anyone else from amongst those who are misguided, on account of his mastery in spiritual works and states. He is indeed one of those men who are managers of the affairs of the women of their egos, and of the affairs of the women of the egos of others as well. Such a perfected person is fit to be a spiritual guide because he can perfect those who are still imperfect by means of the works that he himself initially engaged in while on the path of the lovers (*fī ṭarīq al-muḥibbīn*). He also perfects others with the overflow of his spiritual state, because he has been granted one of the states of those who are near to God after entering from the path of the works of the pious and righteous ones (*min ṭarīq aʿmāl al-abrār al-ṣāliḥīn*). Such a state is fixed and uninterrupted because it has occurred to him after spiritual struggle for which guidance has been promised; God Most High says, *But those who struggle in Our cause, surely We shall guide them in Our ways; and God is with the good-doers* (Q.xxix.69). And since he has become a guide to others, has guided himself and is fixed in his guidance, he is fit to have followers [in search of] guidance, which is transmitted from him to them in the form of spiritual knowledge and states, and which is also generally manifested by the path of the blessings of giving sincere advice.

THE MOST PERFECT STATION IN THE OFFICE OF SPIRITUAL GUIDANCE

Despite such perfection, a man such as this may still have some deficiencies. For he may be confined within his state due to experiencing it after a long pursuit; thus he is at the mercy of his state and comes to a standstill, unwilling to seek any further elevation (*ziyāda*). In this case, he is not released from the shackles of his spiritual state to one that is higher, nor does he reach perfect spiritual giving (*kamāl al-nawāl*) by seeking further elevation. Rather, he stops at his share; and even though such a share is tremendous, it is still a deficiency, because the ranks of the People of Knowledge of God (*Ahl al-ʿIlm bi'Llāh*) are endless.

Therefore, the most perfect station of the office of spiritual guidance is the fourth category of spiritual wayfarers: the spiritually attracted (*majdhūb*). In other words, the one who is loved first, and who is [then] caught by spiritual wayfaring after divine attraction, so he becomes a lover in the second instance, seeking further elevation and not remaining at a standstill in [his] spiritual state. What is meant by being divinely attracted first (*jadhbihi awwalan*) is that, before engaging in spiritual dealing, the Abidingly Real first reveals unveilings to him (which are the lights of certitude) by lifting the tenebrous veils from his heart, and when these are lifted, he becomes illumined by the lights of witnessing (*bi-anwār al-mushāhada*) because of his purity and due to the lack of veils between him and the Abidingly Real.

When the Abidingly Real discloses Himself to him, his heart expands by becoming His mirror (*mirāt lahu*). His heart then expands indefinitely,[1] in the same way that a small mirror would expand to the size of the heavens and earths despite its small original mass. When he becomes a locus of the self-disclosure of the Abidingly Real (*majlī li'l-Ḥaqq*), he turns away from the abode of conceit (*dār al-ghurūr*) due to the manifestation of change in it, and wholeheartedly turns in penitence to the Abode of Eternity (*Dār* al-*Khulūd*) due to the manifestation of lasting pleasures in it. In fact, at that stage, he will drink his fill from the Sea of Communion (*Baḥr al-Wiṣāl*), wherein no consideration is paid to past or future. He will break free from the shackles of worldly attachments, and from shackles that involve turning to anything other than the Master Guardian, with the aim of being realised in witnessing, to the point where he says, 'I do not adore a Lord that I cannot see'; that is, with the eye of certitude (*bi-ʿayn al-yaqīn*). And when he is fully quenched from the Sea of Communion, he will be brought back to spiritual works until he is made a lover in the second instance; thus making his inward aspect overflow into his outward aspect by illuminating it, in the same way that a mirror is illuminated by the light of the sun when it is reflected from a wall or another object.

When a person's outward aspect is illuminated, spiritual struggle (*mujāhada*) runs through him in the form of performing righteous works without him attributing them to himself. He only counts them amongst his works due to the extinction of the ego (*li-fanā' al-nafs*), and, for him, works are [performed] through the unveiling of the oneness of God's Essence, Attributes and Actions. He even

1 This refers to the Prophetic saying narrated by Bayhaqī in *Shuʿab al-īmān* and Ḥākim Naysābūrī in *al-Mustadrak*, vol. IV, p. 346 on the authority of Ibn Masʿūd who reported that the Messenger of God (may God bless him and grant him peace) recited the words of God Most High, *Whomsoever God desires to guide, He expands his breast to Islam* (Q.VI.125), and then said, 'When light enters the breast, it expands.' He was asked, 'O Messenger of God! Is there a sign by which one knows this?' He replied, 'Yes, it is turning away from the abode of conceitedness, turning in penitence to the abode of eternity and readying oneself for death even before it strikes.' However, Dhahabī stated that the chain of transmission of this saying was questionable.

becomes a performer of works through God (*ʿāmilan bi'Llāh*), and God runs them through him to perfect him. That is why they are performed without toil or suffering, just as is the case with Divine Actions that are specifically attributed to God. Instead, he performs these works with joy and happiness insofar as his lights and closeness to God Most High increase through them. And so, he finds his utmost pleasure in this, as pointed out by the Prophet (may God bless him and grant him peace), who said, 'And my utmost pleasure lies in prayer.'[1] In fact, he finds joy in sensory pleasures, too, for his physical form becomes as an attribute of his heart in terms of luminosity, because when his heart becomes filled with the love of his Lord, its love overflows to his physical form, with which the heart has a full relationship. And when the heart's love overflows to the physical form, the latter becomes illuminated by its light. Thus, its earthiness—which implies the difficulty of works that results in toil and suffering—disappears, and the skin softens in the same way that the heart has already softened through the disappearance of the stagnant earthly ego's effect [on it].

The softness of the skin (in other words, the person's outward aspect) is a sign of his inward response to works, since a characteristic of that which is moist is the ease with which it takes on whatever form one wants it to take. That softness follows the softness of the heart that has resulted from its response to the righteous character traits that it was required to embody. All this is insofar as the wayfarer is a lover after being loved by God first, and at this point God Most High will want him specifically after he has been sought by Him through the unveilings that happen to the third category of spiritual wayfarers mentioned above.

This is [brought about] by God distinguishing him with other unveilings, and granting him a special love (*maḥabba khāṣṣa*) from the

1 Narrated by Aḥmad b. Ḥanbal and Abū Yaʿla in their respective *Musnad*s and it is a well-authenticated Prophetic saying. See Abū Yaʿlā Aḥmad b. ʿAlī b. al-Muthannā, *Musnad Abū Yaʿlā*, ed. Muṣṭafā ʿAbd al-Qādir ʿAtā, Beirut: Dār al-Kutub al-ʿIlmiyya, 1998, vol. VI, p. 237.

love of those who are loved (*min maḥabbat al-maḥbūbīn*). However, when any spiritual wayfarer from the third category is granted love from the love of those who are loved, such love is not special for him. Amongst the secrets of this special love is that whoever is loved with it will always continue on [his spiritual journey], even if he happens to be cut off. It may be that he turns away [from the spiritual path] in such a way that merits his being cut off, but in that case, he would then receive a dispatch impelling him to continue.

The reason for running the form of spiritual struggle through him is to dissipate the soul's stagnation (*jumūd al-nafs*), which makes works burdensome to it. The dissipation of [the soul's] stagnation is through its softening for worship and gaining warmth from the heat of the heart that comes to it, just as the heart itself softened upon receiving the heat of the spirit. The soul then overflows onto the body (*tafīḍu ʿalā al-badan*), the external skin softens and the person finds acts of obedience easy and without any hardship. In consequence, the soul's querulous veins are cut off from the heart because it is full of the love of its Lord. God Most High says, *God has sent down the fairest discourse as a Book, consimilar in its oft-repeated, whereat shiver the skins of those who fear their Lord; then their skins and their hearts soften to the remembrance of God* (Q.xxix.23). God Most High informs us that skins soften just as hearts do. But the softness of heart and skin are not combined, except in the state of the loved one who is besought (*al-maḥbūb al-murād*); otherwise, the soul of the lover would remain stagnant, and this would cause it to toil when engaging in acts of worship.

The proof that the soul's veins contract from the heart, which leads to the softening of the heart, is the following Prophetic report, 'Satan (may God curse him) enquired about the way to reach the heart. It was said to him, "It is forbidden for you to reach the heart. However, the way around this is to reach the soul through the channels of the entangled veins up to the limit of the heart. Then, once you access the veins, you will sweat therein due to the channels' tightness, and your sweat will mix in the same channel as the water of mercy that is perspired by the heart. In this way, your authority will reach the heart; however, I remove these veins from the inward aspect of the heart of whomever I make a prophet or saint, and so his heart becomes sound. In this case, if you were to access the veins, you would reach those that are entangled with the heart and your authority would not reach the heart.'"[1]

One Sufi (may God have mercy on him) wrote, commenting on the above report:

> That is to say that Satan made a request to have free rein over the rational soul (*al-nafs al-nāṭiqa*), which is the heart (*qalb*), in order for him to mislead it himself without any intermediary; but his request was denied. However, God placed roots of attachment that incite one to evil between the heart and the soul, which is the animal spirit, and he gave Satan access to those roots, from where he draws the heart towards the ego's desires.
>
> It was also said to Satan, 'If you access the veins, you will drown in them (in other words, your speech will disappear in them just like the speech of a drowning person) because of the tightness of their channels, and the heart will not notice your discourse as it does not see you. And when you drown in them, the perspiration of your whisperings will surface and your sweat will mix with the water of mercy, which is the heart's emanation that arises from the heart's love of the soul. The heart will then confuse your discourse with the discourse of

1 This is not a Prophetic saying and we have not been able to locate its source.

the soul, and this will enable your authority to reach the heart through the return of something from the soul to the heart.'

God (glorified and exalted is He) then said to Satan, 'I remove these veins from the heart's inward aspect of whomever I make into a prophet or saint, so that his inclination towards the ego ceases, except in relation to the emanation upon which its subsistence depends. And so those veins remain by dint of the manifestation of the heart's emanation upon the soul, but the location of the reflection of the soul's vestiges does not remain. This is the location of the outward aspect returning to the inward aspect due to its removal from that location. That is because the soul of such a person becomes at peace and does not incite one to evil, which means that nothing is transmitted from it except the like of that which has overflowed into it. At that point, the heart becomes free from the turbidity of the ego, and whenever you [Satan] access the veins, you will drown and your discourse will also drown, so you will not reach the soul's veins that are entangled with the heart because of their being uprooted and unable to subsist in that respect. Thus, your authority will not reach the heart.'

And it is to this that God Most High alluded with His words, *Surely over My servants thou shalt have no authority* (Q.xvii.65).

And God knows best the realities of matters.

THE STATE OF THE BESOUGHT BELOVED

In sum, the besought beloved (*al-maḥbūb al-murād*)—whether he was first a lover later caught by divine attraction, or was first a loved one who was later caught by spiritual wayfaring after divine attraction—is someone whose heart has been spared from these entangled veins. He is someone whose breast (*ṣadruhu*), which is the locus of his soul, has been expanded because it is free of those veins that pull towards the strait of attachment to the realm of sensory matters. He is also someone whose skin has softened; hence his heart becomes obedient to the spirit because of its union with the heart's face in the ascent to the Higher World. And even if the heart were to turn one of its two faces towards the soul (*nafs*), as long as [the heart] overflows onto [the soul] in doing so, this will not prevent [the heart] from ascending.

The besought beloved is also someone whose inciting soul is obedient to the heart when it eradicates its qualities that incite one to evil, by means of the light emanating from the heart on the pure path of the sound heart. By means of the light emanating from the heart, his soul also softens after being stagnant, after being inclined to lowly matters, inciting to evil and after experiencing great difficulty in ascending to the higher side. His skin has also softened enough that it becomes easy for him to engage in acts of worship due to the softness of the soul that emanates upon the outward aspect. He will be returned to the forms of works after experiencing the spiritual state where his perfection lies. Then his spirit will keep being pulled towards the Divine Presence by the changing of spiritual states and stations over him, with each state and station being purer than the one before. Thus, in its gradual rising, the spirit will make the heart follow it by means of the authority that it has over it once it has reached perfect firm-footedness, because the heart is the spirit's vizier.

In turn, the heart will cause the soul (which is active) to follow it; while the soul will cause the heart (which encompasses all of the other dependent body parts) to follow it. Thus, the works of the heart in terms of superior gifts become mixed with the overall works of sincere acts of worship. Likewise, the outward aspect penetrates the inward aspect by adding to the illumination of the outward through its acts of worship in favour of the inward. The inward aspect also penetrates the outward aspect by softening acts of worship; while Divine Power—in other words, the World of Inward Ultimate Reality—penetrates into the World of Outward Causality (*ʿĀlam al-Ḥikma*), and vice versa. For such a person, the shares of worldly life in terms of sensual desires will turn into joy of the Afterlife in terms of perfect gnosis, while the Afterlife is reflected back into his worldly life through his absorption in Divine Love.

Thereafter, spiritual verities (*ḥaqā'iq*) are revealed to him in a most perfect manner to the point where it would be admissible for him to say what ʿAlī b. Abī Ṭālib (may God ennoble his face) said; namely, 'Were the covering to be lifted, my certitude would not increase further.' In other words, *rather, I would perhaps increase in clarity*. When such a person's unveiling becomes perfect, he is released from the shackles of spiritual states and is no longer restricted by any one state. He has authority over spiritual states—not the other way round; thus, he becomes free in every respect.

ELABORATION OF THE STATES OF THE SPIRITUAL WAYFARER

The first shaykh mentioned in the third category [of spiritual wayfarers]—who was the one who trod the path of the lovers first, and then later became loved; [and who,] when his [ego] is extinguished, is freed from the ego's captivity until he comes upon spiritual states—may remain a captive to his heart insofar as he remains dominated by spiritual states. We say, *may* remain so, because he is connected to the fourth category on account of the fact that spiritual states do not dominate him; instead, he dominates them. This is the shaykh who is first caught in the way of the lovers and is then brought back to the establishment of works, freed from the captivity of the heart so that he is not veiled from created beings by the Abidingly Real, or from the Abidingly Real by created beings. This is because the ego (*nafs*) is a tenebrous veil (*ḥijāb ẓulmānī*) that veils one from the Abidingly Real by means of created beings, from which the shaykh who is first a lover, and later becomes overwhelmed by spiritual states, is freed from its captivity. The heart (*qalb*), on the other hand, is a luminous veil (*ḥijāb nūrānī*) that veils one from created beings by the Abidingly Real, as its gaze is confined to the Higher World. The second shaykh is freed from this also; for he is not veiled from anything, by anything, nor is he overwhelmed by spiritual states—let alone the ego.

When he is freed from the captivity of the heart and spiritual states, he becomes sincerely pure for his Lord. And when he is not attached to anything, he worships God sincerely, and with certainty, and believes in Him truly, without any veil. He is then perfected by making all of his body parts and faculties follow suit. At that point, his whole being prostrates before God (in other words, his body, soul and all of the other inward meanings through outward acts of worship), and his inward aspect also endeavours to prostrate before God. His heart then believes in God; a belief resulting from witnessing and beholding, and his tongue acknowledges this belief, just as the Messenger of God (may God bless him and grant him peace) said during his prostration, 'My body and soul have prostrated before You, my heart has believed in You and my tongue has acknowledged You; and here I am before You, O Forgiver of tremendous sins!'[1]

In fact, not even a single hair of his inward, or outward, aspect fails to show its servanthood, because luminosity dominates over them to the point where his worship becomes akin to that of the

1 Narrated by Bazzār in his *Musnad* with a good chain of transmission as stated by al-Ḥāfiẓ al-Haythamī in *Majmaʿ al-zawā'id wa-manbaʿ al-fawā'id*, Beirut: Mu'assasat al-Maʿārif, 1986, vol. II, p. 152. The saying was also mentioned in Bazzār's *al-Baḥr al-Zakhkhār* and was also narrated by Abū Yaʿlā in his *Musnad*, vol. IV, p. 177.

Angels, performed out of pure joy and encompassing every single part of him. God Most High says, *To God bow all who are in the heavens and the earth, willingly or unwillingly, as do their shadows also in the mornings and the evenings* (Q.xiii.15). In other words, before God prostrate all who are in the heavens of spirits, [all] hearts and their respective soldiers, and all who are upon the earth of souls and their faculties; willingly on the part of hearts and spirits, and unwillingly on the part of souls. However, the prostration in question here follows the nature of the spirits and hearts, and not that of the soul; even if the latter accidentally comes to be at peace.

In this [Qur'ānic] verse, what is meant by 'their shadows' is bodies (*ajsām*), through the coming and going of their manifestation with beauty, or the traits of their manifestation with majesty. Upon the prostration of the spirits, forms prostrate themselves because a shadow does not have an independent action beyond the action of the person to whom it belongs. In the physical world, the basis is solid whereas its shadow is subtle; but the opposite is true in the World of the Unseen, for [there] the basis is subtle whereas its shadow is solid. This is because a shadow in the physical world is akin to a lack of a locus's illumination, and the nothingness that results from its non-manifestation suits subtle lights. And a shadow in the World of the Unseen is akin to the illumination of a locus by means of the shadow's light, [which] makes [the locus] manifest. And manifestation suits subtle matters. As for the shadow that has a shadow, this is in order to manifest it. Manifestation suits solid matters, so the servant's subtlety (which consists of his spirit, heart and soul) prostrates itself, as does his solidity (which consists of his body), such that nothing in him fails to worship in the first place.

Such perfection is not the lot of someone who treads the path of the lovers, if he is a spiritual wayfarer who has been touched by divine attraction, and thus restricted by spiritual states; and the latter dominate over him, because he distastes the forms of works, as he deems them to be a distraction from spiritual states. Consequently, he deems it fit to do without them in order to fill himself with that which he is made to obtain of the experience of spiritual states. He therefore does not perform any works other than those that are obligatory, or regular supererogatory works that he cannot do without, because doing so would vitiate and darken his outward aspect. If this happens, he fears that darkness will then seep into his inward aspect and extinguish the light of his spiritual states. Nonetheless, forgoing other supererogatory works is a deficiency on his part concerning knowledge of the realities of works and their impact on perfecting spiritual states, and also on effecting his lack of any ulterior motives in these states. Had his knowledge of spiritual verities been great, he would have been able to see spiritual states as spirits and works as vessels. He would also have been able to realise that works are connected to spiritual states in the same way that the spirit is connected to the body.

The spirit's acquisition of its perfections depends on the body: when its connection to the body is suspended, it cannot subsequently acquire any further perfection, causing it to stop at the point that it has reached. But were he to possess a great deal of knowledge about spiritual verities, then he would realise that works are indispensable for perfecting spiritual states—in fact, he would preserve them in order to spare himself from being completely pushed back down, just as vessels in the physical world are indispensable for acquiring perfections of this knowledge, which would benefit him forever.

As long as the vessels remain, work will continue; otherwise, this will completely unbalance the connection between body and spirit. Indeed, this would be the very essence of failure. The Perfected One is not veiled by anything, and he finds pleasure in works because spiritual states are perfected through them. In fact, spiritual states are commensurate with readiness, and the latter happens through works. He will therefore lack readiness if he neglects work. Indeed, the Abode of Spiritual States is the Afterlife, while the Abode of Works is this world. Works are like a tree, and spiritual states are its fruits. There would be no fruits without trees; and if there were, they would not last long.

THE ABSOLUTE SPIRITUAL GUIDE

In sum, the spiritual guide of the third category (mentioned above) is a spiritual guide (*shaykh*) in one respect, but not in another. As for the spiritual guide who satisfies the station mentioned earlier, he belongs to the fourth category. He may also belong to the third category if he becomes like those in the fourth category when he is freed from the shackles of spiritual states and is brought to the forms of works, when his spirit does not stop at any spiritual station or state, as mentioned before. This is the Absolute Spiritual Guide (*al-Shaykh al-Muṭlaq*), for he is at the station of subsistence and is qualified to perfect others on the spiritual path. He is also a Realised Gnostic whose knowledge of spiritual verities has been so perfected that he is not veiled from anything, by anything. He is also the loved one (*maḥbūb*) who has been freed from the captivity of his heart and soul.

He is an absolute spiritual guide because his glance is a cure; as he whose glance does not benefit anyone, his words do not benefit anyone either. His words are also a cure because he is at the spiritual station of subsistence: he talks, and refrains from talking, through God; he sees through God and hears through Him, as reported in the holy saying, 'The servant keeps on drawing to Me with supererogatory works until I love him. When I love him, I am to him hearing, sight, hand, heart and support; through Me he speaks and through Me he sees… '[1]

This quality, however, is not encountered in the lover because he is overpowered by spiritual states and does not see anything except the Abidingly Real in the first place. Indeed, he is veiled by

1 Narrated by Bukhārī, *Ṣaḥīḥ*, no. 6502. The meaning of this saying, rather than its exact wording, is quoted here.

the Abidingly Real from created beings—so how would it possible for him to see these things? By contrast, the beloved mentioned above is not veiled from created beings by the Abidingly Real, or by created beings from the Abidingly Real. He grants whatever he grants through God, and withholds whatever he withholds through God, with no reward in return, or any ulterior motive involved. This is because he has no desire to grant anything, nor does any assistance come to him from withholding anything; it is rather the intent of the Abidingly Real in all that.

The Abidingly Real reveals His intent to him by means of subtle allusions and genuine tried inspiration. He is in things through the intent of God Most High, not his own. He acts through God, and also refrains from action through God. When he knows that God wants him to engage in a praiseworthy form of works, he engages in it through God's intent, and not because the form itself is praiseworthy.

THE FORM OF THE PERFECT OFFICE OF SPIRITUAL GUIDANCE

The same applies to the form of the office of spiritual guidance (*mashyakha*) and the perfection of others on the spiritual path: the absolute shaykh embarks upon this through God's intent, not his own. If you realise this, O desirous seeker, then know that, with regard to this tremendous matter, the desirous seeker needs to keep the company of a perfected spiritual guide who has the ability to perfect others, because divine attraction is very rare. This is why Abū Yazīd [al-Bisṭāmī][1] (may God sanctify his secret) said, 'He who has no master has Satan as his imam.' This saying applies generally, because, as we have mentioned, divine attraction is very rare. Otherwise, it is possible that God Most High might pull a person towards Him and remove his base desires (*hawāhu*) so that Satan does not have any

1 Abū Yazīd Ṭayfūr b. ʿĪsā al-Bisṭāmī was a famous Sufi who was born in Bisṭām (a town located between Khorasan and Iraq) in the year 188/803, and died there in 261/874. See Shaʿrānī, *al-Ṭabaqāt al-kubrā*, vol. 1, pp. 76–77; Ziriklī, *al-Aʿlām*, vol. III, p. 235.

authority over him. But this rarely happens; and that which is rare is as if it were non-existent. Even so, Abū ʿAlī al-Daqqāq[1] (may God sanctify his secret) likened such a person to a tree that grows on its own and was not planted by anyone, in that he only has his reason to refer to in order to ward off his base desire so as to obtain the necessary purity that yields the fruit of suprasensible self-disclosures.

THE NECESSITY OF KEEPING THE COMPANY OF SPIRITUAL MASTERS

These fruits of suprasensible self-disclosures are seldom yielded without a spiritual guide, just as an unattended tree in the wilderness seldom yields fruit. Yet it is still possible for someone without a spiritual guide to obtain essential self-disclosures, just as it remains possible for an unattended tree to bear fruit. However, just as the fruit of an unattended tree does not have the same taste as those growing in tended fields, the essential self-disclosures of someone without a spiritual guide will also be lacking, for he will seldom be able to remedy the finer points of hidden base desire on his own without being taught how his remedies work.

This is because in the disposal of the gnostic over anything, his gnosis has an impact on his disposal over that thing. This is why the taste and quantity of fruits improve when what has been planted is moved from one place to another. The spiritual guide also moves the seeker from one station to another until he embraces noble states.

The Noble Sacred Law (*al-Sharʿ al-Sharīf*) has considered it to be necessary to train a working dog, and has declared the consumption of that which it kills to be lawful. This is because when its kills are done in accordance with its training, they are not done due to the dog following its base desire, but rather on the instigation of the person whose orders it follows. By contrast, the kills of an untrained dog

1 Al-Ḥasan b. ʿAlī b. Muḥammad Abū ʿAlī al-Daqqāq was the master par excellence of the Sufis and the mentor of Abū al-Qāsim al-Qushayrī. He died in the year 406/1015 or 412/1021. See Ṣafadī, *al-Wāfī bi'l-wafayāt*, vol. XII, p. 165.

are unlawful for consumption. This is because, in this latter case, the kills were done with the dog following its base desire, and base desire has had an effect on it by making it unlawful for consumption, just as abstention from base desire has had an effect on the former by making it lawful for consumption.

Similarly, anyone who does not have a teacher (*muʿallim*) will be overpowered by Satan who is the master of base desire (*ustādh al-hawā*). It is unlawful to emulate someone such as this. Often, such a person does not become perfected, nor will have the ability to perfect others. The Gnostics (may God benefit by them) say, 'Whoever has not seen someone successful will not succeed himself.' In other words, the spiritual seeker who does not encounter a spiritual guide who disciplines him will never succeed, because he will be overpowered by his base desire and unable to remove it on his own without any help. They also say, 'A state of being flows from the inward aspect of the spiritual guide to the inward aspect of the seeker in the same manner as a lamp acquires fire from another lamp.'

In sum, if teaching and learning were not beneficial, the Messenger of God (may God bless him and grant him peace) would not have engaged in them with his Companions, who were purer and more perfected than us. The Prophetic Companions received knowledge and propriety regarding everything from the Messenger of God (may God bless him and grant him peace); they did not find sufficiency in their own minds, even though these were perfect. So how can we find sufficiency in our minds when we know that they are deficient? In this context the Gnostics (may God sanctify their secrets) have said, 'Through one glance from his teacher, the seeker may reach what he has not reached with many years of spiritual struggle.'

And what is there to deny about the fact that God Most High, through his omnipotence, grants one of His servants a glance through which [that servant] bestows exalted states on others? Just as God (glorified and exalted is He) has created a kind of snake known as *al-Ṣilāna*, which can kill a person with a single glance, it is not far-fetched [to believe] that, in the glances of some of His special servants, He can place that through which a genuine seeker may instantly acquire his heart's life through living eternally. Rather, this is inevitable, because those snakes are the loci of manifestation of majesty, and they must have their opposite in the form of the loci of manifestation of beauty.

What I used to hear from my master, the Gnostic, the Prophetic descendant al-Ḥusayn b. Imām ʿAbd al-Raḥmān b. Muḥammad al-ʿAydarūs (may God benefit by all of them), alluded to this very point. He used to say that with a single glance, the possessor of the evil eye could instantly cause someone to fall ill, or even die. Likewise, amongst the friends of God there are those who can cause the opposite. And it was probably due to this subtle point that my father, my master, the very learned, the knower of God Most High, Imam Shaykh al-ʿAydarūs[1] (may God benefit by them), was in the habit of benefitting from those who were his superiors and his peers, as well as from those who were inferior to him in knowledge (as I had the chance to observe on numerous occasions). I say, 'probably' (and without any degree of certainty in that) because it is also probable that he did this to quash his precious ego.

THE HIGHEST DISCIPLINE OF THE SOUL

My master, the Prophetic descendant Shaykh ʿAbd al-Qādir al-Jīlānī (may God benefit by him) said, 'Whoever finds good spirits in studying under one of his peers, or who becomes his student, will surely rid his soul of its frivolities. This is the highest discipline of the soul. In fact, it is higher than enduring hunger, staying awake at night or solitude.'

1 The author's father, the prophetic descendant, the distinguished Muṣṭafā b. Shaykh b. Muṣṭafā al-ʿAydarūs, was born in the year 1110/1698. He studied the traditional disciplines with a group of contemporary scholars, among them Shaykh ʿAbd al-Raḥmān b. ʿAbd Allāh for the study of exegesis, *Ḥadīth*, jurisprudence, Sufism and the Arabic language. He died in the year 1164/1750. See Ḥabshī, *ʿIqd al-yawāqīt*, vol. II, p. 104.

THE STATES OF THE SPIRITUAL MASTER WITH A SEEKER

You should know, O seeker, that the spiritual seeker with a spiritual guide has a time of suckling, during which he derives benefit from him, and a time of weaning. The spiritual guide knows this very well, but the seeker should not leave his spiritual guide based on the assumption that he has reached the time of weaning, unless his spiritual guide permits him to do so. This is because the time of spiritual weaning is often unclear to the seeker on account of his deficiency. The spiritual guide does not permit the seeker to leave him until he knows for certain that the seeker has reached the time of weaning and can be independent. Such independence consists of opening the door of understanding from God by reaching the station of the spirit and the station of the heart, and seeing of the base desires and turbidity of the ego that which necessitates his thoughts, until he is hardly wrong about anything.

However, this is not the case regarding some matters. Rather, when the spiritual seeker is able to place all his needs and preoccupations through God Most High, along with understanding from Him by means of His indications and warnings, and displaying the utmost humiliation and indigence towards God before doing all this, only then does he reach the time of weaning. If he were to leave his spiritual guide before this, his departure would cause his ego to spring into life and regain its dominance. Teeming spiritual diseases would subsequently overtake him, to the point where he would revert back to this world and follow base desire, in the same way that a prematurely weaned child of a natural birth experiences heaviness of food and indigestion.

When the spiritual guide sees that a seeker is doltish, or otherwise fears for him, he points him towards outward spiritual works and the service of other fellow seekers in order to gain their blessing. And each one finds ease in pursuing that for which one was created. It is to the likes of such a person that it was said, 'Hold fast to the faith of those advanced in years.' In any event, the person who loves people but is unable to do as they do has the rank of God's With-ness alongside them, even though this is true in one respect but not in another. As for the words of the poet (may God have mercy on him) who said:

> You disobey God while pretending to love Him;
> This, by my life, is a singular analogy!
> Had your love been genuine you would have obeyed Him;
> Indeed, the lover is obedient to [He] whom he loves.

Here, there is an indication of deficiency, not negation; so understand!

On Remembrance

EACH FORM OF REMEMBRANCE HAS A PARTICULAR ILLUMINATION

You should also know that because each form of remembrance (*dhikr*) has a particular illumination (*tanwīr khāṣṣ*), a group of Gnostics (may God benefit by them) have chosen one form of remembrance that combines all of the different forms of remembrance for the seeker; namely, the expression, 'There is no deity except God' (*lā ilāha illā Allāh*). This is because this expression possesses a tremendous peculiarity in illuminating the inward aspect through the disclosure of Divine Unity (*al-Waḥda al-Ilāḥiyya*) with singular Divine Oneness (*al-Tawḥīd al-Khāṣṣ*), which is the highest aim beyond which there is no [further] target to reach, nor any [higher] point of rising to rise to, even though such a disclosure occurs in different shapes that vary from pure to purer ad infinitum.

The spiritual seeker must keep repeating this expression with his tongue with the concurrence of his heart, for without this concurrence it would have no significant impact, even though it would not be entirely devoid of benefit. He should not confine himself to the remembrance of the heart from the start, for remembrance through this expression has a facet towards the physical world, and this will distract him from undulated remembrance through which one turns towards the Higher World. When he sees the physical world coming to him, his turning towards the Higher World is completed to the point where he becomes entirely cut off from the physical world. At that point, the expression of 'There is no deity except God' becomes deep-rooted and firm in the heart. And when it is connected in him, it averts the inner speech of the soul from him because its radiance removes the darkness of the soul, which means that its meaning replaces the inner speech of the soul, just as the light of day replaces the darkness of night. And when the radiance of the heart overwhelms him, the seeker apprehends the beauty of 'There is no deity except God,' and its joy dominates him until it overtakes the heart. The effect of this overtaking then spreads over to the outward aspect and it grows easy on the tongue, which is then able to utter it without any difficulty.

The heart then absorbs this expression and experiences its savour, making it impossible for one to leave off repeating it—even when the tongue stops uttering it. At that point, remembrance through this expression becomes engraved upon the heart, and the heart's essence takes on the hue of this expression; the heart is as if it were the remembrance, and the remembrance is as if it were the heart. Through the crystallisation of this expression in the heart, the light of certitude settles there, for this light is akin to one of the accidents of this expression when it becomes a substance. However, substances do not cease on account of the cessation of their forms; thus, when the form of this expression ceases from upon the tongue and in the heart, its light (which is necessary for it to become a substance) does not disappear. When its luminosity is completed, the heart perceives the tremendousness of He Who is Remembered; the expression is engraved upon his limpid substance and remembrance becomes one with beholding the tremendousness of He Who is Remembered, in the same way that a form reflected in a mirror becomes one with the mirror.

And when [the seeker] is united with the tremendousness of He Who is Remembered, it is as if His Remembrance (glorified and exalted is He) is His Essence, through His Essence, in His Essence. This crystallisation is the highest goal, and it is for its sake that the genuine ones take to their retreats; rather than being for the sake of acquiring miracles, or breaking the norms of nature.

HEALING THE INDISPOSITION OF THE INVOKER'S TEMPERAMENT

You should also know that the luminosity of remembrance burns away the attributes of the servant and stirs the heat of his nature by indisposing the soul from its normal nature. Hence, when the spiritual seeker fears harm, by indisposing his temperament, he should mix his constant remembrance with invoking blessings upon the beloved Prophet (may God bless him and grant him peace) by saying, 'Muḥammad is the Messenger of God, may God bless him, his Companions and household, and grant them peace.' This is because invoking blessings and peace on the Prophet (may God bless him and grant him peace) is like water: it strengthens the soul in obeying God Most High and removes the flare of innate natures. It was to this that Abū Bakr al-Ṣiddīq (may God be well pleased with him) alluded when he said, 'Invoking blessings and peace upon Muḥammad (may God bless him and grant him peace) is more effective in blotting out sins than cold water is in putting out fire.' Ibn ʿAṭāʾ Allāh al-Shādhilī[1] (may God benefit by him) mentioned in his work, *The Key to Salvation* (Miftāḥ al-falāḥ), that the sign of spiritual illumination is the eruption of heat in the inward aspect; and a Sufi added that thirst helps in this process.

1 Tāj al-Dīn Aḥmad b. Muḥammad b. ʿAbd al-Karīm b. ʿAṭāʾ Allāh al-Iskandarī al-Mālikī, the great Sufi and educator has numerous works to his name, including *al-Ḥikam al-ʿAṭāʾiyya* and *Laṭāʾif al-minan fī manāqib al-shaykh Abī al-ʿAbbās al-Mursī wa-shaykhihi al-shādhilī Abī Ḥasan*. He died in Cairo in the year 707/1307 and was buried in al-Qarāfa. See Shaʿrānī, *al-Ṭabaqāt al-kubrā*, vol. II, p. 20 and Ziriklī, *al-Aʿlām*, vol. I, p. 222.

THE MANNER OF THE CRYSTALLISATION OF THE QUR'ĀN IN THE HEART

You should know that the aforementioned light may also be crystallised—not by remembrance through the expression, 'There is no deity except God', but by the recitation of the Qur'ān, in which case it is called the crystallisation of the light of speech. This happens when the seeker recites the Qur'ān in abundance, making a great effort to make the heart concur with the tongue during the process, by tallying the meanings with the words that are recited until the heart is completely focused on the meanings and oblivious of the tongue's utterance of the words. In this instance, the heart pays such little attention to the inner speech of the soul that the recitation runs unintentionally on the tongue and Divine Speech replaces the inner speech of the soul due to the heart's [state of] absorption. The heart thus finds joy in this, and the savour of this joy seeps into the soul and body, causing the servant to find ease in his recitation of the Qur'ān and his performance of the prayer due to the soul's heaviness and traits disappearing. The soul's turbidity is thus expunged and its traits are replaced until the inward aspect becomes luminous from the ease experienced in reciting the Qur'ān and performing the prayer through the light of the outward aspect (*nūr al-ẓāhir*) simultaneously pervading the inward aspect (*bāṭin*) with the light of the inward aspect (*nūr al-bāṭin*).

When the light of meanings in the inward aspect is combined with the light of uttered words in the outward aspect, coupled with the light of prayer, Divine Speech becomes crystallised in the heart and the effect of this crystallisation is similar to the effect of the crystallisation of the expression, 'There is no deity except God.' The light of Divine Speech gathers in the heart in tandem with beholding the tremendousness of the Speaker (may He be exalted and glorified), and this leads to unveiling, witnessing and beholding the Divine.

THE SECRETS AND WONDERS OF PRAYER

You should also know, O desirous seeker, that in every single posture of the canonical prayer—indeed, in every single movement that leads to these postures—God has secrets and points of wisdom that lead to amazing spiritual states and wondrous spiritual stations, which are not found in any other common form of invocation.

The best proof of this is the great attention that the most perfect of all perfected created beings (may God bless him and grant him peace) paid to it during his retreats and periods of interaction with others. It was he who said, 'And my utmost pleasure lies in the prayer';[1] 'Let us find rest in it, O Bilal!'[2] and, 'The most beloved of works for God Most High is the performance of the prayer at the start of its appointed time.'[3]

Ibn ᶜAbbās (may God be pleased with father and son and have mercy on both) used to say, 'Performing two units of prayer with contemplation is better than praying for an entire night.' One of the friends of God (may God benefit by them) said, 'I saw the Messenger of God (may God bless him and grant him peace) in a dream and I addressed him, "O Messenger of God, give me counsel!" He replied, "Hold fast to the prayer, for I have asked my Lord to counsel me and He enjoined me to hold fast to the prayer." He said to me, "I am closest to you when you are praying."' And because the Prophetic descendant Shaykh ᶜAlawī b. Muḥammad

1 Narrated by Aḥmad b. Ḥanbal and Abū Yaᶜlā in their respective *Musnads* and it is a well-authenticated Prophetic saying. See *Musnad Abū Yaᶜlā*, vol. VI, p. 237.

2 Narrated by Abū Dā'ūd, '*Bāb ṣalāt al-ᶜatama*,' in *Sunan*, *Kitāb al-adab* and by Dāraquṭnī in *Kitab al-ᶜIlal*.

3 Narrated by Bukhārī, '*Bāb al-ṣalāt*,' in *Ṣaḥīḥ al-Bukhārī*, *Kitāb mawāqīt al-ṣalāt*, nos. 527 and 5970 and Muslim, '*Bāb al-īmān afḍal al-aᶜmāl*,' *Ṣaḥīḥ Muslim*, *Kitāb al-īmān*, no. 85.

Mawlā al-Duwayla[1] (may God benefit by him) was realised in his spiritual inheritance of his grandfather (the chosen one—may God bless him and grant him peace), he used to say, 'The prayer is my greatest delight'; and whenever a matter weighed upon him, he stood and performed the prayer.

THE STATE OF THE ONE IN WHOSE HEART REMEMBRANCE AND THE QUR'ĀN HAVE CRYSTALLISED

You should also know, O desirous seeker, that during the process of progressing with remembrance and recitation of the Qur'ān mentioned above, until the wayfarer reaches the extent of the verity of remembrance and recitation (that is, the crystallisation of their light in union with beholding the tremendousness of the One remembered), he may disappear in remembrance or recitation when his inward aspect becomes pure due to the perfect intimacy he experiences in his remembrance caused by the delight he finds therein. He therefore savours a certain sweetness whose extent can only be appreciated by somebody who has been made to taste it by God. In such an absence, the wayfarer—like a sleeping person—is close to the state of extinction, for the one who is overwhelmed by pleasure is also like this, as it happens upon full ejaculation during sexual intercourse, which meets the conditions of fulfilling the climax of one's pleasure.

When he becomes just like a sleeping person, his outward sensory faculties are suspended and his inward faculties head towards the World of the Unseen after being directed to the physical world. The soul is then divested of the veils of outward sensory faculties and ceases to turn towards the physical world; thus, it runs parallel to the World of the Unseen. At this point, suprasensible verities are revealed

1 He was the first of the honoured ancestors of the Bā ʿAlawī family. He was born in the city of Tarim in Hadramawt. He memorised the Qur'ān (and he was a companion of his father, Muḥammad, and Shaykh ʿAbd al-Raḥmān al-Saqqāf, his brother) and he practised it incessantly until he was trained, then he practised different kinds of obedience until good signs were revealed to him. He died in the year 778/1376. See Shillī, *al-Mashraʿ al-rawī*, vol. II, pp. 209–210.

to him as abstract meanings in imaginal forms, from which he can cross over to these meanings in the same way that abstract meanings are revealed to the sleeping person in the forms of his imagination, such as the revelation of conquering one's enemies in the form of killing a snake—in which case the interpreter of the dream would say, 'You are going to conquer your enemy, by way of crossing over from this form to the abstract meaning.'

CLEAR UNVEILING

When he rises above that, he will obtain clear spiritual unveiling (*al-kashf al-ṣarīḥ*), in that verities will be revealed to him without the garb of similitude by means of which he crosses over to these verities. This is superior to imaginal unveiling (*al-kashf al-khayālī*), for it is an unveiling without the intermediary of similitude. The former unveiling may happen by seeing the similitude of an event in its form in the outside, or it may happen by hearing a call in a disembodied voice (*hātif*) emanating from his inward aspect, from the air, or from something else.

This is as far as wakefulness is concerned. As for when he is asleep, he sees the verities of things without their imaginal garbs, so he sees them like the light of the breaking dawn,[1] as reported by ʿĀ'isha[2] (may God be well pleased with her) concerning the Prophet (may God bless him and grant him peace). So understand this and be guided!

A NOTE OF WARNING. Keep in mind, O desirous seeker, that the wayfarer should not stop at savouring the sweetness (*ḥalāwa*) that he encounters, or be happy with it or descend to it—whether this sweetness is like that which has been mentioned above, or another known, adulterated sweetness—unless this entails spurring the servants to persevere

1 Aḥmad b. ʿAlī b. Ḥajar al-ʿAsqalānī, *Fatḥ al-Bārī bi-sharḥ Ṣaḥīḥ al-Bukhārī*, Beirut: Dār Ṣādir, [no date], vol. 1, p. 23.

2 This is amongst the famous traditions that were transmitted by Bukhārī; see *Ṣaḥīḥ al-Bukhārī*, *Kitāb bad' al-waḥy*, no. 3.

in their acts of worship; namely, that which is experienced in some acts of worship by those who have not reached the station alluded to above. Likewise, his intention in performing spiritual works should not be to acquire such sweetness on account of what it contains in terms of pleasure and portion, because this would lessen the sincerity of his worship (*ikhlāṣ ʿibādatihi*) and the genuineness of his will (*wa-ṣidq irādatihi*). He should rather be keen for this to happen in order to use it simply as a yardstick with which to judge his works, and as a measure of his states. Wāsiṭī[1] (may God benefit by him) said, 'Finding the savour of sweetness in acts of obedience is a mortal poison.' Ibn ʿAṭā' Allāh said in *The Subtle Blessings* (Laṭā'if al-minan), 'Wāsiṭī is right: the least that can happen is that when you experience sweetness during acts of obedience, you become engrossed in it and long to savour more of it; and in so doing, you fall short of true sincerity by rising to perform these acts. You may also like to prolong the savour of such sweetness—not out of observance of loyalty, but due to the savour of sweetness and the enjoyment that you experience. Thus, it would appear as though you were performing these acts for the sake of God Most High; although in truth, you are only following your ulterior motives. It should therefore be feared that the sweetness that you experience during acts of obedience may become a reward that you hastened to take in this world, while on the Day of Judgement you will arrive without any reward.'[2]

THE SIGN OF UNADULTERATED SWEETNESS

The sign of unadulterated sweetness (*al-ḥalāwa al-ghayr al-madkhūla*) is what one Gnostic (may God benefit by him) said, 'To neglect a

1 Imam Abū Bakr Muḥammad b. Mūsā al-Wāsiṭī was a disciple of Junayd and Thawrī. He hailed from Fergana but lived in Khorasan. He died in the year 331/942. See Shaʿrānī, *al-Ṭabaqāt al-kubrā*, vol. I, pp. 99–100 and Ziriklī, *al-Aʿlām*, vol. VII, p. 117.

2 Ibn ʿAṭā' Allāh, *Laṭā'if al-minan fī manāqib al-shaykh Abī al-ʿAbbās al-Mursī wa-shaykhihi al-shādhilī Abī Ḥasan*, ed. ʿAbd al-Ḥalīm Maḥmūd, Cairo: Maṭbaʿat al-Iḥsān, [no date], p. 304.

matter amounts to having very little knowledge of that matter, for disobedience is unlikely while possessing knowledge. But if a Gnostic slips or lapses in relation to a legal ruling, *and God's commandment is doom decreed* (Q.xxxiii.39), he will inevitably feel the consequences of that in the form of bitterness (*marāra*) and suffering (*alam*) in his heart. The experience of such bitterness and suffering upon committing an act of disobedience is a sign of the soundness of the sweetness that he has experienced.'

I have already dwelt at length on the two kinds of sweetness that are experienced in my commentary on some of the inspired sayings of the Prophetic descendant Shaykh al-ᶜAydarūs Abū Bakr (may God benefit by him). This commentary is of about twenty quires [in length] and is entitled, *The Clear Conquest from the Breaths of ᶜAydarūs Fakhr al-Dīn* (al-Fatḥ al-mubīn min anfās al-ᶜAydarūs Fakhr al-Dīn), and may be consulted by anyone wishing to know more.[1]

THE STATES OF THE GNOSTICS

You should also know, O desirous seeker, that the Gnostics (may God benefit by them) have amazing states upon engaging in the recitation of the Qur'ān or in remembrance (*dhikr*). And as the Prophetic descendant Shaykh ᶜUmar al-Miḥḍār ᶜAlawī (may God benefit by him) said, 'When the righteous recite the Qur'ān, they erase the letters and sounds. Then they stand by a sea and then that sea vanishes, so they remain suspended in mid-air in a state of awe and exultation.' And then he added, 'And we are amongst these ones.'

Likewise, my master, Shaykh Saᶜd b. ᶜAlī, the companion of ᶜAydarūs (may God benefit by both of them), often melted upon reciting the Qur'ān to the point where his body became like solidified water. One of the People of Spiritual Unveiling also used to hear, while sleeping, the remembrance of my master, the Prophetic

1 *The Clear Conquest* (al-Fatḥ al-mubīn) was the largest of his commentaries on the poem (*qaṣīda*) of Imam Abū Bakr b. ᶜAbd Allāh al-ᶜAydarūs al-ᶜAdanī, and he wrote two other commentaries on this poem.

descendant Shaykh ʿAbd al-Raḥmān al-Saqqāf's heart, through every single hair and pore of his skin. Even his clothes were heard making remembrance like children in a Qur'ānic school.

The father of the aforementioned Saqqāf, my master the Prophetic descendant Muḥammad Mawlā al-Duwayla ʿAlawī (may God benefit by him), used to say, 'We may make remembrance with the tongue and heart, then we make the letters disappear, and then we make the sound disappear, and what remains in the heart is a candle of light connected to God Most High.'

The Prophetic descendant, my master, Shaykh Muḥammad Jamāl al-Layl ʿAlawī[1] (may God benefit by him), used to say, 'Making the letters disappear upon reciting the Qur'ān is easy for us; unlike making the sounds disappear.' He also used to say, 'When the heart is purified, it cannot get enough of the recitation of the Qur'ān.' And upon reciting the Qur'ān, he used to say, 'How sweet is this; its sweetness is unlike that of sugar, honey, or anything else.'

My master, Shaykh Miḥḍār, who was mentioned above, used to repeat: 'O Benevolent One (*yā Laṭīf*)', 1000 times in a single breath, while one of his servants used to repeat it 500 times in a single breath.

It also happened that my master, the Prophetic descendant Shaykh ʿAydarūs Abū Bakr (may God benefit by him), recited the whole Qur'ān one thousand times over in a single day. It is he who said in one of his precious spiritual insights in verse, 'As for me, my whole being is engaged in Your remembrance / And all my body

1 Muḥammad b. Ḥasan al-Muʿallam b. Muḥammad Asad Allāh b. Ḥasan b. ʿAlī, son of the Foremost Jurisprudent (*al-Faqīh al-Muqaddam*). He had two *laqabs*: al-Shayba and Jamāl al-Layl. He was born in the city of Tarim in the year 750/1349. He memorised the Qur'ān and was a companion of his father and his paternal uncle, Aḥmad. He studied jurisprudence and studied with the scholars of his time in *Ḥadīth*, exegesis and Sufism. He used to live in a village known as Rawgha. He died in the year 845/1441 and was buried in Zanbal cemetery; his tomb there is still visited. See Shillī, *al-Mashraʿ al-rawī*, vol. 1, pp. 177–179.

parts are eyes for You.' One of the scholars of his time experienced a spiritual unveiling about this and saw that Shaykh ʿAydarūs was all tongues engaged in remembrance with eyes gazing.

Similarly, one of the greatest Gnostics, who had ample knowledge of the esoteric and exoteric disciplines, used to make remembrance of 'There is no deity except God (*lā ilāha illā Allāh*)' at all times. When he slept, people used to hear him making the same remembrance in his sleep. This same Gnostic used to say, 'The swiftest forms of remembrance for obtaining results are "There is no deity except God" and the recitation of *Sūrat al-Ikhlāṣ* (Q.CXII). Had I known the secrets contained in "There is no deity except God" at the beginning of my spiritual wayfaring, I would not have sought any other knowledge except it.' Another Sufi used to be devoted to remembrance through the formula, 'God (*Allāh*).' One day, a plank [of wood] fell on his head, and the blood that spilled onto the ground took the shape of the word 'God.' Similarly, when the limbs of Ḥallāj (may God benefit by him) were cut into pieces while he was nailed to a cross, his blood took the shape of the word 'God' on the ground. He said about this, 'Not one limb or joint is cut off from me / Except that I have remembrance of You in it!'

The Prophetic descendant, my master Shaykh ʿAbd Allāh b. Shaykh ʿAydarūs, the resident of Shahar (may God benefit by him), was asked to explain why something like this did not happen to the martyred Imam Ḥusayn (may God be well pleased with him), even though he was undoubtedly and undisputedly much higher in spiritual station and state than Ḥallāj. His response was that Ḥallāj was killed on the presumption of his killer that he was an unbeliever, so God made his innocence manifest through what [subsequently] happened to him. On the other hand, Imam Ḥusayn was not killed due that [same] presumption. In killing him, his killers were committing a sin both outwardly and inwardly. What drove them to resist him—even though they knew who he was—was nothing but oppression, resentful envy and tyranny. By contrast, those who killed Ḥallāj had some kind of excuse and justification [for their actions]. In fact, they were right to kill him as they applied the outward purport of the Sacred Law.

In this, they followed the example of our master Moses (peace be upon him) in his protests against the actions of Khiḍr (peace be upon him). However, there is some deficiency in such a stance, since it only takes into consideration the outward purport of the Sacred Law. It is for this reason that our Prophet (may God bless him and grant him peace) said regarding our master Moses (peace be upon him), 'If only he had been patient!' This is because it is possible to understand the words of the Gnostics as being correct from both the standpoint of reason (*ʿaql*[an]) and the Sacred Law (*Sharʿ*[an]), as advanced by Abū Ḥāmid al-Ghazālī (may God benefit by him), who said concerning Ḥallāj, who had said, 'I am the Abidingly Real (*anā al-Ḥaqq*),' that, 'He was completely absorbed in the Abidingly Real to the extent that there was no room in him for anyone else. And that which encompasses the entirety of a thing and absorbs it completely may be said to *be* that thing.'

THE HEAT OF REMEMBRANCE

Consider here what Ibn ʿAṭā' Allāh has said regarding remembrance, for it is truly of the gift of God:[1]

> Remembrance is a raging and unstoppable fire, which, upon entering an abode says, 'I, and nobody else!' It is amongst the meanings of 'There is no deity except God.' And so, when it finds wood in it, it burns it; if it finds darkness, it becomes light and illumines it; and if it finds light in it, it becomes light upon light.

1 Ibn ʿAṭā' Allāh al-Iskandarī, *Miftāḥ al-falāḥ wa-miṣbāḥ al-arwāḥ fī dhikr Allāh al-Karīm al-Fattāḥ*, ed. Muḥammad Ibrāhīm, Beirut: Dār al-Kutub al-ʿIlmiyya, [no date], p. 8.

Remembrance eliminates the surplus parts of the body that are a result of excessive food, or the consumption of unlawful food. As for what results from that which is lawful, it is necessary for the body. When the unwholesome parts are burned away and the wholesome parts remain, you will hear remembrance from each part of the body like the blowing of trumpets. The first remembrance takes place in the globe of the head, and in it, you experience a sound like that of the trumpet.

REMEMBRANCE IS A SULTAN. When it sets camp in a place, it does so with all his trumpets and cymbals. This is because remembrance is the opposite of everything that is other than the Abidingly Real. Hence, when it lands in a place it engages in the negation of all its opposites, just like when water comes into contact with fire. After the sounds mentioned above, you will hear different sounds like the ripple of water, the blowing of wind, the sound of fire as it blazes, the sound of the grinding of millstones, the gallop of horses and the sound of tree leaves rustling when moved by the wind.

This is because a human being is a compound (*murakkab*) [consisting] of every precious and lowly subtle substance (*jawhar*) of earth, water, fire and air, [as well as] that which lies in between heaven and earth. These sounds are the invocations of each principle (*aṣl*) and element (*ʿunṣur*) of these substances. Whoever hears any of these sounds has glorified and exalted God

Most High with every tongue, which is the result of the remembrance of the tongue with complete focus.

The servant may even reach a situation whereby if he stops making remembrance, his heart moves within his breast like the movement of a foetus in its mother's womb, demanding remembrance. They [the Sufis] say, 'The heart is like Jesus son of Mary (may peace be upon both) and remembrance is its milk.' When it grows and gains power, it emits sounds and thundering out of longing for remembrance and for Him Who is remembered. The remembrance of the heart resembles the buzzing of bees, for it is neither loud and distracting, nor silent and unnoticed.

THE FORM OF REMEMBRANCE THAT COMBINES ALL SPECIAL PROPERTIES

Amongst those who used to have a litany (*wird*) was he who recited the remembrance (*dhikr*) 'There is no deity except God' seventy thousand [times] on each day of congregation—this form of remembrance [combining] the special properties (*khawāṣṣ*) of all other forms of remembrance—namely, my master, the Prophetic descendant Shaykh Aḥmad b. Abī Bakr al-Sakrān,[1] the brother of ʿAydarūs (may God benefit by them). Likewise, our master, Shaykh

1 Aḥmad b. Abī Bakr b. ʿAbd al-Raḥmān al-Saqqāf was born in Tarim. He memorised the Qur'ān in his infancy and, while still very young, studied the religious disciplines with his father, who also initiated his son into the Sufi path. He was well known for his renunciation and self-contentment. He died in the village of al-Lask in the year 869/1464, and was buried in the Zanbal cemetery in Tarim. See Shillī, *al-Mashraʿ al-rawī*, vol. II, p. 50.

ʿAlī b. Abī Bakr,[1] the brother of al-ʿAydarūs, used to mention this form of remembrance in abundance day and night. It is he who said in some of his inspired sayings in verse, 'We have a secret in the expression of Divine Oneness / And in its oft-repeatedness there is a tremendous treasure.'

Similarly, our master, the Prophetic descendant ʿAbd Allāh Bāḥusayn al-Saqqāf ʿAlawī[2] (may God benefit by him), used to repeat 'There is no deity except God' seventy thousand times a day when he was just seven years old. It is he who said in one of his inspired sayings in verse, 'The remembrance of God is my food and drink / And remembrance of God is my conquest of lands.'

THE STATES OF ECSTASY

You should know and always keep in mind, O desirous seeker, that whenever you experience ecstasy (*wajd*), the commotion that ensues in you is one of three things: (1) if your commotion is due to overwhelming fear (*khawf*), then you will be like someone who trembles and cannot control his shivering; (2) if it is due to overwhelming hope (*rajāʾ*), then your commotion will be like a sneeze that you cannot suppress, for one expects nimbleness from sneezing; or (3) if it is due to overwhelming exhilaration (*faraḥ*) and ecstasy (*wijdān*), then the commotion will be like that of a breath that a breathing person necessarily exhales, since this happens upon being exhilarated.

In all of these examples, complete compulsion (*al-iḍṭirār al-kullī*)

1 Shaykh Nūr al-Dīn Abū al- Ḥasan ʿAlī b. Abī Bakr b. al-Shaykh ʿAbd al-Raḥmān al-Saqqāf was born in Tarim in the year 818/1415, where he was raised and learned to memorise the Qurʾān. He was known for his fondness of the books of Abū Hamid al-Ghazālī. He travelled in pursuit of knowledge to Shahar, Aden, Zabid, Mecca and Medina. When he finally returned to his birthplace, he occupied himself with teaching until he died in the year 895/1489. He was buried in the Zanbal cemetery and his grave is still visited. See Shillī, *al-Mashraʿ al-rawī*, vol. II, pp. 215–218.

2 The noble Prophetic descendent ʿAbd Allāh b. ʿAlī Bāḥusayn al-Saqqāf al-Makkī has several publications to his name, including *Īḍāḥ al-kashf al-akbar*, *Kitāb al-nafas al-Raḥmānī*, *Tanbīh al-sālikīn* and others. He died in the year 1152/1739. See Shillī, *al-Mashraʿ al-rawī*, vol. II, pp. 215–218.

and complete absence (*al-ghayba al-kulliyya*) are not prerequisites, for a feverish person may experience some trembling without losing consciousness. Yes, it is true that some who are in ecstasy experience complete absence—as happened to the father of my master ᶜAyadarus, my master the Pole and Prophetic descendant Shaykh Abū Bakr al-Sakrān b. ᶜAbd al-Raḥmān al-Saqqāf (may God benefit by both), who did not sleep day or night for eleven months and spent most of his nights during this period in spiritual audition (*samāᶜ*). People of Spiritual Audition also came to him in this period every Friday between the times of *ᶜAṣr* and *Maghrib* prayers to deliver their auditions, and he would circle around them in the streets. During those months, he walked as if inebriated. He also visited the knower of God Most High, Sulṭāna Bint ᶜAlī al-Zubaydī[1] (may God benefit by her), to whom his visit was disclosed (*kāshafat*) before he even reached her town, and she told those around her, 'Go welcome the king, the son of a king, for I have heard the gatekeeper in heaven announce his arrival. I can see the Angels bid him farewell, and he is accompanied by a huge crowd of people.' Then after that, he (may God benefit by him) denied all of the things that he had done during those months, including sessions of spiritual audition, visiting Sulṭāna Bint ᶜAlī al-Zubaydī and walking around in the streets. He said, 'I would not have done any of those things had I been aware of what I was doing.'

The like of this does indeed happen a great deal. Whoever takes the trouble to trace similar events that happen to the friends of God Most High in the right sources will find them in abundance. However, most of those who experience ecstasy are like the ones we mentioned first. Nonetheless, such people would be hurt if they were to be stopped from moving, for the scream of the ecstatic per-

1 Shaykha Sulṭāna Bint ᶜAlī al-Zubaydiyya, a Sufi and a religious preacher, was born in the year 780/1378. She was well known for her righteousness and renunciation, and is known to have composed some poetry. She died in the year 847/1443. See Muḥammad b. Aḥmad al-Shāṭirī, *Adwār ta'rīkh al-ḥaḍramī*, Medina: Dār al-Muhājir, 1392/1972, vol. II, p. 308.

son allows him to breathe. And even though this breathing is due to some kind of volition (*irāda*), that volition is compulsory in one respect, so it is enough that there is some kind of compulsion; the remaining element of choice being of no consequence. Otherwise, were the ecstatic person to hold back and suppress himself, this would lead to his harm or complete destruction, both of which are prohibited (*ḥarām*). So understand!

On Retreat

THE TYPES OF SINCERE WAYFARERS IN ENTERING RETREAT

You should also know that the sincere wayfarers (*ṣādiqīn*) who enter spiritual retreat (*khalwa*) are of two kinds: (1) the spiritual wayfarer who is a lover (*muḥibb*) and (2) the spiritual wayfarer who is a loved one (*maḥbūb*).

THE LOVER. The spiritual wayfarer who is a lover (*muḥibb*) enters spiritual retreat against the wishes of his ego (which incites one to evil) so that he may achieve sincerity (*ikhlāṣ*) and truthfulness (*ṣidq*). He does so against the wishes of his ego because it hates retreat by nature, since this deprives it of mixing with people. By nature, the ego is inclined to mix with others because its desires (*shahawātahā*) cannot be fulfilled except through this. However, in most cases, mixing with others prevents one from performing the core acts of worship (*aṣl al-ʿibādāt*). And if one were to perform them, one's ego would mostly prompt one to engage in showing off, hypocrisy and in all others sins and wanton desires.

When the disciple (*murīd*) disrupts the ego from the habits to which it has grown accustomed since childhood, which is [done] by confining it in one place in the obedience of God Most High, it feels pain because that runs against its exigency. At each moment of the retreat, the ego tastes bitterness, which brings sweetness to the heart because, by nature, the heart (*qalb*) is inclined to the Sublime Refuge (*al-Janāb al-ʿUlwī*), whereas the ego (*nafs*) is inclined to the lower realm (*al-janāb al-suflī*), which [in turn] goes against the heart's nature. However, it may so happen that, with the help of Satan (to whom the ego is a student), the ego gains the upper hand over the heart and pulls the heart towards its side. So when the disciple makes the ego taste the bitterness of acts of obedience, its pull weakens, and this allows the heart to return to the requirements of its nature and thereby taste the sweetness of acts of obedience. The more that he tastes of this sweetness, the more he will love sincerity and truthfulness upon their performance, such that his acts of obedience become sound. The wayfarer who is a lover (*muḥibb*) wants that which he loves to be sound, and when he tastes the sweetness of acts of obedience, these acts become beloved to him, and therefore he wishes for them to be sound.

THE CONDITIONS FOR A PERFECT SPIRITUAL RETREAT

O desirous seeker, you should also realise that spiritual retreat (*khalwa*) is not perfect unless your name is removed from amongst the people [without a trace]. This erasure happens when you no longer savour people's opinion about you due to having abandoning them by stopping your inward aspect from facing them, or turning towards them or towards what they say about you. Instead, you should face the wall of your retreat and concern yourself with nothing but the matter at hand until your soul is completely annihilated. This is because solitude (*waḥda*) and retreat (*khalwa*) lead to extinction (*fanā'*); indeed, they lead to all of the spiritual stations, from beginning to end.

THE LOVED ONE. As for the spiritual wayfarer who is a loved one (*maḥbūb*), he is the one who feels an urge in his inward aspect (in other words, in his spirit or heart) to enter spiritual retreat, so his peaceful soul (*nafsuhu al-muṭma'inna*) is willingly attracted to it. This is more complete on the part of his ego because it lacks the element of inciting one to evil, and it is more perfect on the part of his heart because it does not contain any of the turbidity of the soul, and it is also proof of the perfect readiness of his spirit (*rūḥihi*) in that he is fit for the Divine Presence without the intermediary of a prior acquisition. This state—that is, the state of being beloved (*ḥālat al-maḥbūbiyya*)—was the state of the Most Beloved (*Ḥabīb*), the Messenger of God (God bless him and grant him peace), for there are reports of his state that indicate that this was so.[1]

And you should know that it was related from the Prophet (may God bless him and grant him peace) on the authority of ʿAbd Allāh b. Masʿūd (may God be well pleased with him) that he said, 'A time will come for people when one's religion will not be safe for the person who has religion, except for he who flees with his religion from township to township, from mountaintop to mountaintop, and from one hole to another, exactly like a chased and frightened fox.' He was asked, 'When will this happen, O Messenger of God?' He replied, 'When a means of living cannot gained except by disobeying God. When such a time comes, celibacy will become widespread.' He was asked, 'How so, O Messenger of God, when you have commanded us to marry?' He replied, 'When that time comes, the destruction of a man will come at the hands of his parents; if he does not have parents, then his destruction will come at the hands of his spouse and children; and if he does not have a spouse or children, then his destruction will come at the hands of his relatives.' Again he was asked, 'How so, O Messenger of God?' He replied, 'They will rebuke him for his constrained means of living, and this will push him to commit that which he cannot bear until it leads him to destruction.'[2]

1 That is, when he used to retreat to the cave of Ḥirāʾ for days and nights at a time, as reported by Bukhārī in his collection of rigorously authenticated Prophetic sayings; see *Ṣaḥīḥ al-Bukhārī*, *Kitāb badʾ al-waḥy*, no. 3.

2 Narrated by Khaṭṭābī in *Kitāb al-ʿUzla*, from the report of Ibn Masʿūd, who attributed it to the Prophet (may God bless him and grant him peace); it was also narrated by Bayhaqī in *Kitāb al-Zuhd*, from the report of Abū Hurayra, who attributed it to the Prophet (may God bless him and grant him peace); and also by Rāfiʿī in *Taʾrīkh Qazwīn*. This Prophetic saying is weak (*ḍaʿīf*).

THE HARMS OF MIXING WITH PEOPLE

One of the Knowers of God (may God benefit by him), who commented on the above Prophetic saying, wrote:

> That is to say that a time will come for people when one's religion will not be safe for the person who has religion due to the evil of those who surround him; from amongst his family, children, relatives, friends and others who believe him to be perfected when he has not yet reached perfection. When this happens, conceit (*ʿujb*) and showing off (*riyāʾ*) will take hold of him. Those who will be safe from this are those who flee from township to township with their religion, and who, if they cannot do so, [flee] from mountaintop to mountaintop, and who, if they cannot do [that either], then cloak themselves with the garb of common people and move from one hole to another like a fox who is afraid of everything.
>
> He was asked, 'When will this happen, O Messenger of God?' And he replied, 'When a living is not earned except by disobeying God.' In other words, by being a tyrannical ruler, a corrupt or ignorant judge, an overseer of endowments or trusts who betrays the trust placed in him, or someone who seeks to become close to those in power by falsely denouncing another person, through iniquity, or by acquiring that which is unlawful. When this happens, sedition (*fitna*) will spread amongst the people and none will be fit to be taken as a companion. And if there were

someone who was fit to be taken as a companion, he will hardly be free from seeing himself as someone of consequence and will appoint himself as people's mentor before being qualified to be so, driven by an empty claim and self-delusion.

Then the Prophet (may God bless him and grant him peace) said that when such a time comes, there will be no form of companionship whatsoever between people, to the point where celibacy (which is sometimes an obligation, and sometimes an act of imitation of Prophetic practice) will become widespread, so that marriage takes place in instances where it is neither obligatory nor praiseworthy. He was asked how this turn of events could happen when he had already commanded them to marry (sometimes as an obligatory act, and sometimes as a praiseworthy act), and his ruling may not be abrogated after him. He answered them that marriage would be vitiated because its harms would outweigh its benefits, and just as the command to marry would no longer apply at that point, so too the rights of one's parents and the right to maintain ties of kinship would no longer apply. This is because when that time comes, a man's destruction will be at the hands of his parents; if he does not have parents, then his destruction will be at the hand of his spouse and children; and if he does not have a spouse and children, then his destruction will be at the hand of his relatives.

Again, the Prophet (may God bless him

> and grant him peace) was asked how could this possibly happen when obedience to parents was one of the greatest acts of perfection enjoined by God (glorified and exalted is He)—Who said (and as other texts have said), *Thy Lord has decreed you shall not serve any but Him* (Q.XVII.23)—and likewise ties of kinship and marriage through which [arise] the orderliness of the world, and the abandonment of which [bring about] the ruin of the world? He responded by saying that it was true that all of these things were highly commendable, but that they were vitiated by the mere fact of being rebuked for one's constrained means of living because this would lead to failures that cannot be mended by the perfections of those commendable acts, and a man would fail to earn his livelihood by lawful means until he met his destruction.

How excellent is our Shaykh, the Prophetic descendant, the eminent Jaᶜfar al- Ṣādiq, the son of the Knower of God Most High Muḥammad al-Baytī ᶜAlawī (may God benefit by him), who said in verse:

> Intermingling with others is only confusion and an infectious disease,
> And in solitude, I detect levelheadedness.
> A person's reliance on people betrays impotence,
> After what has been revealed in *Sūrat Ṣād* (Q.XXXVIII).

He is referring here to God's words, *And indeed many intermixers do injury one against one another, save those who believe, and do deeds of righteousness—and how few they are*! (Q.XXXVIII.24).

In sum, the intelligent person is his own physician, so let him always keep in mind the words of the Prophet (may God bless him and grant him peace), 'Solitude (*wiḥda*) is better than an evil companion, and a righteous companion is better than solitude.'[1]

How excellent is the one who said:

> A person's solitude is better
> Than having an evil companion with him;
> And a good companion is better
> Than a person's sitting alone.

Our Shaykh, the very learned, the noble ᶜAbd al-Raḥmān b. ᶜAbd Allāh b. Aḥmad Bilfaqīh (may God benefit by him) said in his poem rhyming with 't' (*tā'*): 'There is no point in meeting people except / To reform someone's state or to gain some wisdom.'

THE PERFECTED SPIRITUAL GUIDE AND RETREAT

Spiritual retreat is so important that the Knowers of God (may God benefit by them) said concerning the perfected spiritual guide (*al-shaykh al-kāmil*) who is able to perfect others, that one of the proprieties that the spiritual guide compels himself to follow is to make a special retreat where no created being accompanies him—either externally [that is, physically] or internally [that is, in terms of his inward aspect]—at a special time during which he experiences the utmost purity (*ṣafā'*) and delight (*ladhdha*) in the company of God Most High. At that time during that retreat, he cannot [attain] the stations of companionship (*maqāmāt al-ṣuḥba*) with other created beings—states that necessitate the integration of (*al-jamᶜ bayna*) the Abidingly Real and created beings. [This is] so that he is not veiled from one of them by the other [meaning, being veiled from the Abidingly Real by created beings, and vice versa]. [He should not] even seek help during this retreat as [his state] may overflow onto anyone who is there with him in retreat.

At that special time during his retreat, he is not encompassed by the stations of companionship (*maqāmāt al-ṣuḥba*) with other cre-

1 Narrated by Ḥākim Naysābūrī in *al-Mustadrak*, vol. III, p. 343 and by Bayhaqī in *Shuᶜab al-īmān*; but it is not a sound report (*lā yaṣiḥḥ*).

ated beings in which he must behold the Abidingly Real and created beings at the same time so that he is not veiled by one from the other. The perfected spiritual guide uses spiritual retreat to gain strength in order for his state to overflow into those who are not with him in his retreat.

The perfected spiritual guide should not claim that there is a spiritual power (*quwwa rūḥāniyya*) within himself that exempts him from having to resort to retreat due to the fact that he sees himself as being above being veiled by the Abidingly Real from created beings, or by created beings from the Abidingly Real. He should not make such a claim lest he think that keeping prolonged company with people—especially if it is through talking to them—would not harm him in that the veils would be drawn over him, or that his spiritual state would be affected and diminished to begin with. This is because, by making such a claim, he thinks that he does not need retreat because his interaction with people (*jalwatihi*) is itself a retreat; when in reality, the matter is the opposite of what he thinks. To exist completely without the veil of people is a very lofty state, which is extremely difficult to sustain even in retreat—let alone while talking to them (which gradually brings him back down to the limits of humanity). Then again, how could this claim and this opinion about his perfection be valid when one knows that the most perfected of all created beings (may God bless him and grant him peace) himself resorted to retreats?

THE NECESSITY OF SPIRITUAL RETREAT

Even though he reached the utmost perfection, the Messenger of God (may God bless him and grant him peace) made a retreat each night, during which he stood in prayer, made remembrance and meditated. Moreover, he had supererogatory prayers at night and during the day that he diligently observed. He also had unspecified times at which he would retreat for self-purification (*bi'l-taṣfiya*) due to the lingering of human nature (*ṭabᶜ al-bashar*) in him, which tends to become turbid without careful management (*siyāsa*). Human nature can hardly do without careful management to prevent turbidity, whether the remnants of this human nature are great or small, and regardless of whether this nature is subtle or solid. [And the need for managing the human nature is] due to the fact that the integrated human constitution (*al-jamʿiyya al-insāniyya*) requires [the human nature] to remain in some way or another. And if the human nature persists, then it must inevitably be managed. This is because if [the human nature] remains in some specific way or another, but there is no management [of it], then it will inevitably emerge in other [more serious] ways—just as when a small fire is not carefully observed or put out, it flares up and spreads—and since it is inevitable that human nature exists, its careful management is thus imperative.

A CAUTION ABOUT CLAIMS CONCERNING THE WELL-BEING OF THE HEART

How many [a man] has been deceived [into acting in a certain way for the sake of] the well-being of the heart (*ṭībat al-qalb*), dispensing himself from the need to manage his nature (*ṭabʿ*), being content with the ease (*bi'l-yasīr*) [that comes] from [acting for the sake of] the well-being of the heart, using it as his [spiritual] capital (*ra's mālihi*), and pretending that it is the universal goal of all acts of worship and spiritual retreat. Thus, deluded by the well-being of his heart, he becomes oblivious to the management of his human nature, which leads him to relinquish restraint in jesting and interacting with people, until his ego gains the upper hand and he makes a claim to the office of spiritual guidance on the basis of this presumed well-being. He, therefore, appoints himself to the office of spiritual guidance, without actually providing any guidance, and makes himself an example to those idle ones who waste their time and do not pay heed to what they do. To help himself in this process, he provides food for people and treats them kindly, while not bothering with the obligatory statutes [of God] (*bi'l-ʿazā'im*). In consequence, those who go to him are those who are after food and gentleness—not those whose aim is religion or treading the Path of the Godfearing (*Ṭarīq al-Muttaqīn*), the Masters of the Obligatory Statutes [of God] (*Arbāb al-ʿAzā'im*). Such a claim becomes a trial for him, and his claim to the office of spiritual guidance will lead people astray. The least that can happen to him is that he remains deficient, and unable to rise through lofty stations. How can it be otherwise when he has fallen into the clutches of languor in works, whereas he is supposed to be a knight of wayfaring through spiritual states and stations?

POVERTY AND RETURNING TO GOD DURING RETREAT

If human nature always remains (as we have indicated), then the spiritual guide cannot do without summoning succour from God Most High, just as a human being cannot do without eating every day, since what has been eaten in the past is not of any help in sustaining him if he abstains from food for a long time due to the elapse of that past time which can cause his human nature to dissolve. This summon of succour is made by humbly entreating God Most High through his heart, if not through both his heart and whole body, for every single word that he has uttered to created beings, he should return to God Most High in his retreat and he should display humble submission before Him. This does not come readily to a person who mixes and talks continuously with people unless he renews himself through a light in his inward aspect (*bi-nūr fī bāṭinihi*) whenever any aspect of their darkness (*ẓulmatihim*) befalls him. This is because mixing and talking with people inevitably make the ego (*nafs*) grow stronger, even if some time has passed since [interacting with them].

Sedition (*fitna*) calling for one to abandon retreat and to act despicably by [confining oneself to just] outward acts of worship only enters upon those who are deluded into [acting for the sake of] the well-being of the ego, and who claim to possess a spiritual power that is not contradicted by anything that requires spiritual retreat to the point where they have abandoned restraint in talking with others without returning to God Most High, and have engaged in excessive jesting without committing themselves to spiritual retreats. They have ignored the fact that the ego can emerge upon the slightest help that is consistent with its base desires. They have also been deluded by possessing some talent without knowing that preserving this talent is extremely difficult when one throws off all restraint; indeed, this is impossible for most people. Their lack of knowledge of the ego's traits and their delusion are due to their lack of emulation of the perfected, perfecting spiritual masters amongst the Predecessors (*Salaf*). They have imagined that, because it has been extinguished, the ego has therefore been completely abolished; but this is far from being the case. Instead, all that happens is that the ego is no longer felt, and if not, then it remains in one's inward aspect (*fī al-bāṭin*). It is therefore necessary to carefully manage it, and to not do without what we have mentioned above, unless one can find something else beneficial with which to replace it, as Junayd (may God benefit by him) said to his students, 'If I knew that performing two units of prayer were better than sitting with you, I would not have sat down. This is because sitting with you is only good to the same extent as it is beneficial for guidance (*irshād*), which is better than supererogatory acts of worship (*nawāfil*): "That God guides one single man through you is better for you than red camels."[1] The Prophet (may God bless him and grant him peace) said this to ʿAlī (may God ennoble his face). Thus, if [my sitting with you] is not for the purpose of spiritual guidance, then it has no meaning.'

LANGUOR AND HOW TO DEAL WITH IT

If the matter is indeed as we have described, then the perfected spir-

1 Narrated by Bukhārī, '*Bāb faḍl man aslama ʿalā yadayhi rajul,*' in *Ṣaḥīḥ al-Bukhārī, Kitāb al-jihād wa'l-sayr*, no. 3009 and by Muslim in '*Bāb min faḍā'il ʿAlī b. Abī Ṭālib,*' *Ṣaḥīḥ Muslim, Kitāb faḍā'il al-Ṣaḥāba*, no. 2406.

itual guide will choose retreat when he thinks that retreat is better, since in that case, interaction with people would only be officiousness. And if he thinks that sitting with people would be better because it is for the sake of spiritual guidance, then he will opt to sit with his companions who are his brothers on the spiritual path. If, on the other hand, he thinks that it would be better to make a retreat and interact with his students at the same time, then he will opt for both. [And the reason why he would want to interact with them at all is that this] saves his retreat from tediousness [by providing him with] some beneficial liveliness. [Then he may] return to his retreat enlivened, resulting in [his] perfecting [his retreat] out of longing for it. And, [reciprocally,] his retreat augments his interaction with his students. In other words, [it augments it] because of the benefit [that comes] to social interaction from guidance stemming from the light of retreat (*nūr al-khalwa*).

Indeed, there is a subtle point here in that the human being consists of a compound constitution (*dhū tarkīb mukhtalif*) wherein there is opposition (*taḍādd*) and differentiation (*taghāyur*). Due to this differentiation, he has a share of languor in relation to being steadfast in administering that which is right and true. It is for this reason that each agent or actor (*ʿāmil*) has an inward or outward languor (*fatra ẓāhira aw bāṭina*), as this languor may relate to the form of work, so that he does not do any works at all, or it may relate to a failure to find any enjoyment in work; and when languor does not relate to the form of work, he may work without experiencing any enjoyment in it. Now, if languor is inevitable, it becomes even clearer that it turns completely against the deficient person because there is no share of worship for the deficient person during his languor—or for anyone else, as he will use this period to entertain his ego and to submit to idleness. When this happens, the ego (*nafs*) becomes heavy (*thaqīla*), recalcitrant (*jāmiḥa*), inclined to evil (*mayyāla ilā al-sharr*) and undesirous of returning again to the retreat, as though it had been saved from fire and thus hates to return to it.

THE CONDUCT OF THE PERFECTED ONE IN THE STATE OF LANGUOR

When the perfected [spiritual guide] (*kāmil*) has gained this great insight (in other words, that languor usually leads to seeking entertainment and embracing idleness), he becomes extremely wary of it. The person who has reached the perfection of the office of spiritual guidance devotes the period of his languor to guiding people. Thus, other created beings gain success from his share of languor; and what an act of worship this is! The loss incurred due to the spiritual guide's share of languor is unlike the loss incurred by the deficient seeker, whose languor becomes a means of strengthening his ego. And if the loss incurred through languor causes the ego to gain strength, then the deficient seeker returns from languor to devotion to God in his retreat with a strong ego that vehemently demands its base desire, whereas the perfected spiritual guide gains another virtue for his soul from his languor, which is benefitting people. Thus, he returns to his devotion to God Most High in his retreat, which feeds his particular state with eagerness to do so because it brings him the virtue of benefitting others. As his languor has not caused his ego to seek further avidity or base desire, the spiritual guide longs for retreat more than the seeker when he returns from languor to retreat, even if this occurs with a vehement will, as a willingness to return to retreat is opposed by the ego's avidity and its seeking of base desire.

And if the spiritual guide's longing to retreat were greater, then he would return from the company of created beings to his retreat without any languor and with an eager heart full of light, with a spirit free of the constriction of alterity, directed as he has been to serving his zeal for the Abode of Permanence (*Dār al-Qarār*), which is seeing the absoluteness of the Abidingly Real (*iṭlāq al-Ḥaqq*) in retreat.

Imam Ghazālī (may God benefit by him) alluded to some of this when he wrote, 'Because worship is the means of salvation, and because peoples' natures are innately disposed to weariness (*sa'āma*), different litanies (*al-awrād al-mukhtalifa*) have been prescribed so that by varying them one eradicates this weariness.'

Shaykh Muḥyī al-Dīn b. ʿArabī (may God benefit by him) also said, 'The reciter of the Qur'ān never grows weary due to the different meanings mentioned in it.'

THE RETREAT OF THE MASTERS OF INSIGHT

How beautiful are the following words of one Gnostic (may God benefit by him) about the meaning and importance of retreat:

> People say, 'Open your eyes and observe the signs (*ʿibar*) and vestiges (*āthār*) so that from them you may cross to the One Who has caused them.' I, on the other hand, say, 'Close your eyes so that you do not see them, for they may distract you from the One Who has caused them, and behold the One Who has caused them Himself without the intermediary of crossing from the vestiges to Him!' And if this beholding is by means of vestiges, then seeing the latter in the soul (*fī al-nafs*) will be more complete than seeing them on the horizons, for it is indeed due to this that God Most High mentioned the souls last in His words, *We shall show them Our signs on the horizons and in themselves* (Q.XLI.53).

This is what drove one Gnostic (may God benefit by him) to say:

> God has servants whose ascents—which draw them close to the degrees of prophethood (*darajāt al-nubuwwa*)—are their knees, upon which they place their heads in a state

> of watchfulness when they are in the loci of God's proximity (*maḥallāt al-qurb*), asking for more. As for anyone for whom the source of life from the water of proximity (*mā' maʿīn ḥayāt al-qurb*) springs up in the darkness of his retreat, veiling him from sensory matters, he has no need to enter the darkness that Khiḍr (peace be upon him) entered to obtain his goal; nor has he any need for the darkness of peregrination (*ẓulamāt al-safar*), which will not add one iota to what he has already gained.
>
> And anyone for whom the levels of the heavens have been folded up [like a book] in his beholding of the Abidingly Real Who encompasses all, he has no need for turning his glance towards the heavens, when what he has already gained includes that, in addition to an infinity of other things. Anyone for whom the character traits of his insight (*akhlāq baṣīratihi*) have gathered all of the diversified created beings together at the station of the Divine Presence (*maqām al-Ḥaḍra*) has nothing to gain from traversing vast open countries. The perception of insight (*baṣīra*) is more comprehensive and truer than the perception of physical sight (*baṣar*), for physical sight only perceives that which it turns towards, and often it errs.

From this, the secret behind the practices of the Naqshbandī Sufi Order (*al-ṭarīqa al-Naqshbandiyya*) will become clear to you, and why it has been said that it is the closest Sufi order to God Most High, as we have clearly indicated in our epistle on this Sufi order entitled, *The Gift of the Friend on the Sublime and Beautiful Drink* (Itḥāf al-khalīl fī al-mashrab al-jalīl al-jamīl).

SATAN IS A HIGHWAY ROBBER

And you should know, O desirous seeker, that Satan may come to you during your retreat, or in other instances when you are engaged in acts of worship, and will whisper to you, 'You are showing off in your works' in order to stop you from performing those works. You should answer him by repeating what one of the Gnostics (may God benefit by them) said to him, 'The performer of works (*ʿāmil*) who shows off is better than the sincere person who is idle (*al-mukhliṣ al-baṭṭāl*).' For when spiritual works are continuous, they necessarily engender a light that instantly makes them sincere. If, on the other hand, you try to nullify Satan's whispering with an elaborate argument to refute his notion, you will only end up allowing it to firmly implant itself in your soul on account of its antecedence and the depiction of its form in the imagination.

Thus, by means of this it will become clear to you that warding off such thoughts is only possible by [firstly] accepting them, and then [secondly] distracting oneself from them by occupying yourself with their opposite whenever they emerge. It is due to this that Sufyān al-Thawrī[1] (may God be well pleased with him) said, 'If Satan comes to you while you are engaged in prayer and says to you, "You are showing off", then offer him more of it by prolonging the prayer even further.' The Prophet (may God bless him and grant him peace) said, 'Praise be to God Who has reduced his [Satan's] guile to just whispering.' It is also said that Satan is like a dog; when you resist him, he tears animal hides to shreds and tears up clothes. But if you address his master, then [his master] will gently lead him away from you.

1 Abū ʿAbd Allāh Sufyān b. Saʿīd b. Masrūq al-Thawrī al-Kūfī was a master of *Ḥadīth* and an expert in many disciplines of the Sacred Law. He was born in Kufa in the year 97/715, and died in Basra in the year 161/777. He is the author of *al-Jāmiʿ al-kabīr*, *al-Jāmiʿ al-ṣaghīr* and *Kitāb al-farā'iḍ*. See Muḥammad b. Aḥmad b. ʿUthmān, al- Dhahabī, *Siyar aʿlām al-nubalā'*, ed. Shuʿayb al-Arna'ūt et al., Beirut: Mu'asasat al-Risāla, 1985, vol.VII, pp. 229–279; Ṣafadī, *al-Wāfī bi'l-wafayāt*, vol. XV, p. 278; Shaʿrānī, *al-Ṭabaqāt al-kubrā*, vol. I, p. 47; and Ziriklī, *al- Aʿlām*, vol. III, p. 104.

It has been reported that one night Satan went to a Gnostic (may God benefit by him) while he was engaged in prayer, and whispered to him that he was showing off. The Gnostic tried to ward off this thought with several counterarguments, but the thought persisted until God inspired him to accept the thought and then expel it from all of his works by saying, 'Affirmation that I am showing off in this present work is affirmation that I am sincere in others. All of my works are deficient, and this is all that is in my power to do.' Then Satan's whispering left me instantly. Praise be to God.

On the Manners of the Disciple

THE WISDOM OF PERFORMING ACTS THAT BREAK THE NORMS OF NATURE

And you should know, O desirous seeker, that God may reveal verities (*ḥaqā'iq*), and grant occurrences that break the norms of nature (*khawāriq*), to some people in order to strengthen their certitude and thereby benefit them. However, they will only benefit from these if they accept them with propriety (*bi-adab*), if they do not stop at them, or fear God's devising and luring one to destruction because of them, and if they avoid haughtiness towards those to whom these things have not been granted. This is because there are those to whom the unveiling of verities and breaking of the norms of nature have not been granted, and yet these people are far superior to those to whom they have been granted, because they have been granted to serve as intermediaries to strengthen the seeker's certitude in his Lord on the condition that they neither veil nor disconnect him from his Lord.

Whoever is granted pure certitude in his Lord does not need any of the things mentioned above, as verities in themselves do not veil him, whereas breaking the norms of nature cut him off from his Lord. And even when they do not harm him at all, they still do not benefit him either, unless he rises to a station where nothing veils him from anything else—which is the station of the crystallisation of the light of remembrance or recitation of the Qur'ān (*maqām tajawhur nūr al-dhikr aw al-tilāwa*) that was mentioned earlier. The one who reaches this station beholds the Abidingly Real with His attributes, which include His knowledge and power, and so he knows Him (*fa-yaʿlamuhu*) through His knowledge (*bi-ʿilmihi*) and has power (*yaqdiruhu*) through His power (*bi-qudratihi*). It is indeed to this that Imam Ghazālī (may God benefit by him) alluded when he wrote, 'Spiritual states and unveilings are present with you in your heart but you are distracted from them by your attachments and desires, which are veils that separate you from them. All that you require is to break your side [with spiritual struggle] and lift the veil so that the lights of gnosis (*anwār al-maʿārif*) rise from the heart's inward aspect.'

Imam ʿAydarūs (may God benefit by him) said, 'Nothing has veiled the eye of your heart from perception except you. When your darkness has been dissipated from the heart, He Who has always resided in it in the hiddenness of eternity will be disclosed to it.'

ON THE MANNERS OF THE DISCIPLE

You have learned, O seeker, from the preceding [discussion] that the death of the heart (*mawt al-qalb*) is amongst the desires of the ego (*nafs*), and that the life of the heart is proportionate to the extent to which the seeker rejects the ego's desires.

And you should know, O desirous seeker, that amongst the manners of the disciple (*min ādāb al-murīd*) with his spiritual guide is that he should not keep any spiritual event or unveiling to himself without consulting [his spiritual guide]. For due to his lack of knowledge, he may not be in a position to push away what may appear ambiguous to him by not knowing, for instance, whether their source is God or his ego. When he consults his spiritual guide about them, [his spiritual guide] will inform him, for the spiritual guide's knowledge is far more extensive than his. And if he fails to inform him immediately, the spiritual guide will return to God Most High, as his door to God Most High is open wider. If the spiritual event encountered by the disciple is from God, the spiritual guide will concur with him and approve it; and if there is an ambiguity in the spiritual event, in that it resembles what comes from God because it is from the disciple's ego, then the disciple will dispel this ambiguity by consulting his spiritual guide for the latter knows the difference between what emanates from the ego and what emanates from God.

Moreover, by consulting his spiritual guide, the disciple will acquire knowledge through his master's teaching of the validity of future spiritual events and unveilings, which he does not know before consulting his spiritual guide due to his lack of knowledge. The spiritual event experienced by a disciple may coincide with a latent wish in the seeker's ego that drives him to confuse this latent wish with sound unveiling—regardless of whether this happens during sleep or wakefulness.

In this ambiguity there is an amazingly subtle point, in that the soul produces imaginal forms (*al-ṣuwar al-khayāliyya*) when its wish for something overwhelms it, giving the impression that it is as if they had truly happened to the disciple, due to the intensity of [the ego's] desire to get what it wants. This happens a great deal in dreams, and it may happen during wakefulness when the ego is overwhelmed by an intense desire for something to the point of absorption.

THE INTERLACING OF SPIRITUAL STATES AND STATIONS

And one of the things that you ought to know about, O desirous seeker, is the interlacing of spiritual states and stations (*tadākhul al-aḥwāl wa'l-maqāmāt*). That is to say, the seeker cannot complete a spiritual station unless a spiritual state that precedes it descends, for there can be no spiritual station except after an antecedent spiritual state. An example of this is the state of contentment (*ḥāl al-riḍā*), which is the rejoicing of the heart in everything, whether it is sweet or sour. The descent of this spiritual state recurs repeatedly—which here is seeing the perfection of God's actions and mercy, after which the seeker opposes the ego's nature by opting for that which counters its base desire until God's assistance catches up with him and he obtains contentment, which then becomes his station. Thus, the spiritual wayfarer rises through spiritual states to spiritual stations.

Spiritual states—being gifts (*mawāhib*) from the Abidingly Real—become a means for God to influence the wayfarer's departing from spiritual states to spiritual stations. This is because it is correct that some of the Abidingly Real's actions are causes of others (such as making sickness a cause of death, sending down rain for trees to grow, or continuous sinning being the cause for God's vengeance and chastisement). And even if all [of these actions] naturally belong to God, and [although] His actions cannot be explained through causes (*ghayr muʿallala*), [nonetheless,] some of [those actions] are signs for others—just as health is a sign of [one's] continued existence.

THE PERFECTION OF THE WAYFARER'S SPIRITUAL STATION

Likewise, the spiritual station that the wayfarer is in will only be perfected by the descent of the state from the spiritual station above it, because impending spiritual states are a means of confirming the preceding stations. No spiritual station is completely confirmed except through the descent of the spiritual state above it. This is because, in his spiritual station, the wayfarer is granted a state from the station above it to which he will rise. By experiencing that state, the station in which he is presently stabilises. However, it is also possible that the call of one's nature to its exact opposite may materialise. Here is an example: the station of contentment is permanent and judged to be lasting even in the presence of [a person's] nature (*ṭabʿ*), such as the contented person experiencing a certain disgust due to his innate nature. However, due to his knowledge of the station of contentment, the judgement of his nature is suppressed. Thus, the emergence of his nature's judgement in the form of experiencing a suppressed disgust does not deprive this wayfarer of the station of contentment; for what is taken into account is that which is overwhelming, not that which is suppressed, which is like nothing.

Nonetheless, the emergence of [his] nature's judgement in the experiencing of disgust makes the wayfarer lose the state of contentment. This is because spiritual states are never conjoined with the ego, nor do they even mix with it in the first place, just as oil does not mix with water but rather floats on the surface. So thus, the spiritual state never covers the ego. When the ego emerges, it disappears; but when the ego does not emerge, there is no reason for its disappearance. It is therefore called a state (*ḥāl*) because of its changing nature and disappearance (*li-taḥawwulihi wa-zawālihi*), just as a station (*maqām*) is so called because of its permanence and confirmation (*li-thubūtihi wa-istiqrārihi*).

THE PATH TO FINDING THE PERFECTED SPIRITUAL GUIDE

Yes, there are some spiritual states that do not become spiritual stations at all. And if you were to ask, 'Where can I find the perfected, perfecting spiritual guide (*al-murshid al-kāmil al-mukammil*) that you have pointed me to so that I may tread the spiritual path at his hands?' Then my answer would be this. Whoever seeks earnestly will find, and whoever persistently knocks at a door will eventually be allowed to enter. If you were to seek cold water, it would seek you upon thirst; and if a loving, caring mother who has lost a child were to seek him, she would certainly find him. Even if we were to grant that you did not find the perfected spiritual guide, this would only be because you have not yet seen him—not because he does not exist, as pointed out by our master, the very learned, the noble ʿAbd al-Raḥmān, son of the Imām, Shaykh of Shaykhs ʿAbd Allāh b. Aḥmad Bilfaqīh (may God benefit by them), in his poem rhyming in 't' (*tā'*): 'The folk of light, virtue and purity were never scarce, / Scarce, indeed, are eyes that can see.'

My master, Shaykh Abū al-ʿAbbās Aḥmad b. ʿUqba al-Ḥaḍramī,[1] the student of ʿAydarūs (may God benefit by them), used to say, 'Hold fast to continuous remembrance (*dhikr*) and abundant invocation of blessing and peace on the Messenger of God (may God bless him and grant him peace), for it is a staircase and ladder when the seeker has not yet found a spiritual guide.'

THE COUNSELS OF AḤMAD B. MŪSĀ AL-MUSHARRIʿ

Similarly, my master, Shaykh Aḥmad b. Mūsā al-Musharriʿ[2] (may God benefit by both) said:

> Whoever does not have a spiritual guide to discipline him, to make him progress and to take him to God Most High ought to adhere to the invocation of blessings and peace on the Prophet (may God bless him and grant him peace), for it will improve him by means of the best Prophetic manners (*al-ādāb al-nabawiyya*), and refine him with the most noble Muḥammadan character traits (*al-akhlāq al-Muḥammadiyya*), and it will make him ascend to the apex of perfection and reach the most exalted locus in the Presence of the Great and Exalted. It will also gladden him through his beholding of God and

1 Aḥmad b. ʿUqba al-Ḥaḍramī al-Makkī was a Sufi and a scholar. He was the teacher of Shaykh Aḥmad Zarrūq, and the author of several books, including *Ṣudūr al-tartīb*. He died in Cairo in 895/1489. See Zayn al-Dīn Muḥammad b. ʿAbd al-Ra'ūf, al-Munāwī, *al-Tabaqāt al-kubrā aw al-Kawākib al-duriyya fī tarājim al-sāda al-ṣūfiyya*, ed. Muḥammad Adīb Jādir, Beirut: Dār Ṣādir, 1999, vol. III, pp. 138–141 and Sakhāwī, *al-Ḍaw' al-lāmiʿ li-ahl al-qarn al-tāsiʿ*, Beirut: Dār Maktabat al-Ḥayāt, [no date], vol. II, p. 5.

2 Abū al-Qasim al-Junayd Aḥmad b. Mūsā al-Musharriʿ ʿUjayl was a Sufi who withdrew to the vicinity of the two Holy Mosques. He died in Mecca in the year 917/1511 and was buried in Muʿalāt cemetery. See ʿAydarūs, *al-Nūr al-sāfir*, pp. 143–144.

> his proximity to the Prophet (may God bless him and grant him peace).

He used to advise his companions to recite *Sūrat al-Ikhlāṣ* (Q.CXII) and to abundantly invoke blessings and peace upon the Prophet (may God bless him and grant him peace). And he used to say, 'Through the recitation of *Sūrat al-Ikhlāṣ*, I have come to know God the One, the Unique; and through abundantly invoking blessings and peace upon the Messenger of God (may God bless him and grant him peace), I have become his companion.' And he used to say, 'Whoever frequently invokes blessing and peace upon the Messenger of God (may God bless him and grant him peace) will see him during sleep and wakefulness.'

THAT WHICH IS FEARED BY THE SPIRITUAL WAYFARER

So apply that and you will be guided! And you should also know that one of the most feared things for the spiritual wayfarer is that which Imām Ghazālī and other Gnostics (may God benefit by them) warned against. Ghazālī (may God benefit by him) said:

> God (glorified and exalted is He) has seventy veils of light (*sabʿīn ḥijāb*^{an} *min nūr*); the wayfarer does not reach any one of those veils on the spiritual path without believing that he has arrived. The first veil between God and the servant is the heart (*qalb*), for it is a lordly matter, a light from God's light (*nūr min nūr Allāh*), in which all the verity of the Abidingly Real is disclosed until it encompasses and surrounds the whole world, and the forms of all are disclosed in it. When this takes place, the heart's light radiates with such force that the whole world as it is, appears in it. And upon the disclosure of its light, the beauty of the

> heart is revealed. The possessor of such a heart is then so amazed by his heart's extreme beauty that his tongue may slip and says, 'I am the Abidingly Real (*anā al-Ḥaqq*).'
>
> If what is behind this does not become clear to him, he will delude himself with this beauty and stop at it, and perish. It is as though he has been deluded by [nothing but] a small star from amongst the lights of the Divine Presence, when he has not even reached the moon, let alone the sun. Such a person deludes himself. Here lies the ambiguity; for that which is disclosed (*mutajallī*) is obfuscated by the locus of disclosure (*mutajallā fīhi*) in the same way that light reflected in a mirror may be obfuscated and thought to be the mirror's own light; or like when light reflected by glass is thought to emanate from the glass itself. Indeed, it was with such an eye that the Christians looked upon the Messiah (peace be upon him), for they saw the brilliance of God's Light (*Nūr Allāh*) shining in him and so they were mistaken, just as when someone sees the reflection of a star in a mirror, or in the water, thinking that the star is actually in the mirror or water, and so reaches towards it with his hand to touch it, when [in fact] he is simply deluded.

It was mentioned that one of the shaykhs worshipped his spirit for thirty years because of the radiance that he saw from it, which led him to think it was the Abidingly Real. Then the Hand of Divine Care (*Yad al-ʿInāya*) pulled him away from this and he returned to God, Who saved him from this dangerous predicament. May God protect us from everything that takes us away from Him through His pure favour, Amen.

We have dwelt on this topic at length in our commentary, *The Clear Conquest from the Breaths of ʿAydarūs Fakhr al-Dīn* (al-Fatḥ al-mubīn min anfās al-ʿAydarūs Fakhr al-Dīn), so consult it as it will benefit you; and God is Vast and All-Knowing, *Like Him there is naught; He is the All-Hearing, the All-Seeing* (Q.XLII.11). And since we have mentioned the disclosure of God's Essence, Attributes and Actions in a general fashion above, in what follows we shall deal with some of the special properties of those disclosures so that the spiritual wayfarer is made aware of his Lord's Command.

DISCLOSURE BY WAY OF ACTIONS

We say, you should know that disclosure by way of actions (*al-tajallī bi-ṭarīq al-afʿāl*) is a rank of proximity that is higher than the ranks of all the common righteous people, and the divestment of actions from causes is manifested in it. This is because if Divine Oneness (*Tawḥīd*) is in order, then all causes vanish in the fountainhead of all causes (in other words, [the act of] seeing them as being causes vanishes, even though they still exist). As our grandfather, the Prophetic descendant ʿAlī Zayn al-ʿĀbidīn al-ʿAydarūs[1] (may God benefit by him), said to one of his students, 'O ʿUmar! Do not consider actions without [also considering] the Ever-Active One (*Faʿʿāl*), and conceal yourself in Him from the usefulness of wealth and the righteousness of spiritual state.'

What is alluded to here is [the fact] that causes (*asbāb*) are not intermediaries (*wasāʾiṭ*) upon which Divine Action depends. Rather,

1 Shaykh ʿAlī Zayn al-ʿĀbidīn b. ʿAbd Allāh b. Shaykh, son of al-Shaykh ʿAbd Allāh al-ʿAydarūs, was born in Tarim in the year 984/1576. He memorised the Qurʾān and was quick to memorise it with good diction. He grew up under the guardianship of his father, and he practised incessantly day and night until he excelled in the disciplines of his age. He studied the religious sciences with his father, including exegesis, jurisprudence, *Ḥadīth*, Sufism and knowledge of the verities (*ʿilm al-ḥaqāʾiq*). He also studied under a group of other scholars. He died in the year 1041/1631. See Shillī, *al-Mashraʿ al-rawī*, vol. II, pp. 221–227.

God acts at the occasion of these causes (*ʿindahā*), not by means of them (*lā bihā*). In this context, how beautiful are the following words in verse of one of the Gnostics (may God benefit by him):

> When you disappear from time and space,
> And in your mirror existence in unison comes;
> In it you'll see the Causer of all causes
> Causing them, and doing what He wills.
> And you will witness Him as an imagined figure (*khayāl*) when you examine
> Them in themselves, and you will be extinguished by witnessing.
> Disclosure will make you subsistent in each moment,
> For, indeed, you are continuously a new creation.

In these verses there is an allusion to [the fact] that the World of Power (*ʿĀlam al-Qudra*) is also not devoid of causes, but its causes are hidden; as opposed to the World of Causality (*ʿĀlam al-Ḥikma*), where causes are manifest.

The perfected Gnostic, who is divested in the presence of God's action, does not pay attention to causes (whether they be hidden or manifest), for he sees the Abidingly Real as the Actor (*Fāʿil*) in each and every action (*fiʿl*), and does not see anyone else besides Him. To him, God's considerable wisdom in the minutiae and generalities of His actions is manifested, so that he ascertains that there is no ignominy in any of them in relation to God. And were any ugliness or ignominy to appear in any of these actions in the loci of manifestation, then this would be in relation to what is other than God due to their being a sign of His overpowering might and rigour (*ʿalāmat al-qahr wa'l-jalāl*).

Disclosure by way of actions brings about the limpidity of contentment (*ṣafw al-riḍā*), because the Gnostic sees the perfection of Divine Wisdom in things. It also brings about utter submission, lest he protest against God Most High. However, this does not preclude forbidding evil (*al-nahy ʿan al-munkar*), it does not preclude discontentment with disbelief and acts of disobedience nor does it preclude submitting to those who commit them. This is because he accepts these insofar as they are from God Most High, not insofar as they proceed from himself or from others—just as when one finds satisfaction in a person's killing of an enemy, who also happens to be one's own enemy, [and one finds this satisfaction] on account of the destruction of one's enemies; yet [at the same time] one is dissatisfied by this because the destruction of one enemy has strengthened [the position] of the other [since the latter's] enemy was also killed. Or, this can be likened to a person who takes bitter medicine because it will help to heal his disease, even though he dislikes its bitterness, which is repellent to his innate nature.

Disclosure by way of attributes (*al-tajallī bi-ṭarīq al-ṣifāt*) allows one to gain awe (*hayba*) in the disclosure of majesty, and intimacy (*wa'l-uns*) in the disclosure of beauty. Disclosure by essence (*al-tajallī bi-dhāt*) allows one to gain extinction (*fanā'*) whenever one has seen the extinction of everything in the One (*Wāḥid*), and subsistence (*baq ā'*) when one has seen the sustaining of everything by the One by existing through Him.

EXTINCTION

In the terminology of the Gnostics (may God benefit by them), the term, 'extinction' (*fanā'*), is used as a homonym (*mushtarak*). They may use it to refer to the abandonment of choice (*tark al-ikhtiyār*) upon supporting oneself solely with the action of God, as this indicates the extinction of one's will (*irāda*) and also of base desire (*hawā*), as the extinction of the latter implies the extinction of will. This is because the will is the most subtle of the subdivisions of base desire, for if one had not desired it for oneself, one would not have chosen what one chose, nor preferred it to other things. However, such extinction is only outward extinction (*al-fanā' al-ẓāhir*) because the locus of the will is the heart (*qalb*), which is one of the things that are outward in relation to the spirit (*rūḥ*). As for inward extinction (*al-fanā' al-bāṭin*), it consists of the erasure of the vestiges of existence (*maḥw āthār al-wujūd*)—which are the spirit, the heart and the soul—upon the gleaming of the light of witnessing, in that its luminosity in the light of the outward aspect is erased from it in the same way that the light of other stars are erased at the rising of the sun. This occurs during the disclosure of the Divine Essence.

Just as outward extinction upon the disclosure of Divine Actions and the disclosure of the Divine Essence is the most perfect of the subdivisions of certitude in this world, it is also experienced through insight (*bi'l-baṣīra*), not through physical sight (*lā bi'l-baṣar*). As for the disclosure of the judgement of the Divine Essence through physical sight, it has only happened to our Prophet (may God bless him and grant him peace), but it is possible in the abode of the Afterlife. This is, indeed, the station that the Messenger of God (may God bless him and grant him peace) gained during the Night of Ascent (*Laylat al-Miʿrāj*), despite still being in this world, due to acquiring the attributes of the People of the Afterlife, as his luminosity overwhelmed his outward aspect. It is for this reason that the Prophet (may God bless him and grant him peace) did not have any shadow (*ẓill*).

Similarly, disclosure through attributes and actions is like disclosure through the Divine Essence; by which I mean that the aim of all of them is not seeing with the physical eye, but rather detecting one's share of certitude that results from seeing by means of insight. So understand!

Upon mentioning that the Prophet (may God bless him and grant him peace) did not have a shadow, I invoke mercy upon our companion ʿUmar ʿAqīl al-Makkī, who said in verse: 'The world steps into the shade of he who / Has no shadow, and into the alterities that he effaces.'

THE STATION OF EXTINCTION

You should also know that the station of extinction in the Divine Attributes (*maqām al-fanā' fī al-Ṣifāt*) results from the proximity occasioned by supererogatory acts (*nawāfil*); whereas the station of extinction in the Divine Essence (*maqām al-fanā' fī al-Dhāt*) results from the proximity occasioned by obligatory acts (*farā'iḍ*), as is explicitly mentioned in the speech of the Sufis.

A BENEFICIAL NOTE. Know that some people have been confused regarding the words of my master, Zayd b. Aslam[1] (may God benefit by him), who said, 'God (glorified and exalted is He) may love a servant to such an extent that He would say to him, "Do as you will, for I have forgiven you."' [Similarly,] the words of the Prophetic descendant, Shaykh Abū al-Ḥasan al-Shādhilī[2] (may God benefit by him), who said, 'The Friend of God (*Walī*) reaches a point where it is said to him, "We bid safety to accompany you, and we have lifted all blame from you."'

Utterances such as these have proved to be ambiguous for many of the common people, as they believed that when a person reaches the station of love or intimate friendship (*maqām al-maḥabba wa'l-khilla*), he will not be harmed by any sin; whereas in reality, this is not the case. What is meant by such utterances is that when a person has assumed the Character Traits of God (*takhallaqa bi-Akhlāq Allāh*), he reaches a spiritual station called the station of the disposal of power (*maqām taṣrīf al-qudra*)—also called the station of 'be-and-it-is' (*maqām kun fa-yakūn*).

Due to his having realised this station, the Prophetic descen-

1 Imam Abū ʿAbd Allāh Zayd b. Aslam al-ʿAdawī al-ʿUmarī al-Madanī was a jurisprudent and a Qur'ānic exegete, as well as a *Ḥadīth* transmitter. He taught at the Mosque of the Prophet (may God bless him and grant him peace). He died in the year 136/753. See Dhahabī, *Siyar aʿlām al-nubalā'*, vol. v, p. 316 and Ziriklī, *al-Aʿlām*, vol. iii, p. 56.

2 Abū al-Ḥasan ʿAlī b. ʿAbd Allāh b. ʿAbd al-Jabbār al-Shādhilī was a descendant of al- Ḥasan b. ʿAlī b. Abī Ṭālib and Fāṭima al-Zahrā', the daughter of the Messenger of God (may God bless him and grant him peace). He was born in the Maghrib, performed the Pilgrimage several times and died in the desert of ʿAydhab (where he was also buried) on his way to the Pilgrimage during the month of Dhū al-Qiʿda, 656/1258. See Shaʿrānī, *al-Ṭabaqāt al-kubrā*, vol. ii, p. 4.

dant, Shaykh ʿAlawī b. al-Faqīh al-Muqaddam[1] (may God benefit by both) said:

> I say to a thing, 'Be!' and it is, by the leave of God Most High [...] and as ʿAydarūs reported from his Lord that He said to him, 'Do as you will, for I have forgiven you.' And at that moment it is said to him, 'Do as you will, for you have reached this station, and because your burden and the heaviness of existence have been lifted from you, and the illusion of your 'I-ness' (*wahm āniyyatik*) has been completely erased from you. Your state therefore befits this bestowal of honour and this exclusive privilege—not what the common people who are immersed in desires and characterised by their shares of the egos believe.'
>
> In fact my master, Yūsuf b. Asbāṭ[2] (may God benefit by him), said, 'Each person obeys God, and disobeys Him, except the lover [of God; in other words, he can never disobey Him].' Shaykh Abū al-Ḥasan al-Shādhilī (may God benefit by him) said, 'Love refuses to use a lover except for in what agrees with his beloved.'

I say, someone may point the finger of blame at me and reproach me for going on and on in this short commentary as if ignoring why I have mentioned all of these tremendously beneficial points. Which is

1 The prophetic descendant, Shaykh ʿAlawī b. al-Faqīh al-Muqaddam, was born in Tarim and grew up under the care of his father. He was taught by him and he studied the traditional disciplines under him. He died in the year 609/1212 and his grave is known as East Zanbal, the grave of his father. See Ḥabshī, *ʿIqd al-yawāqīt*, vol. II, p. 124.

2 Yūsuf b. Asbāṭ was one of the Sufis of the second/eighth century. He died after the year 190/805. See Shaʿrānī, *al-Ṭabaqāt al-kubrā*, vol. I, pp. 61–62.

to say that he does not understand that the term 'spiritual wayfarer' (*sālik*) drags all these things along with it [by association]; or that everything that I have mentioned needs to be pointed out to the seeker (*ṭālib*) who treads the path of the Abidingly Real, lest he stumble and fall, or slip into heresy. By my life, what we have not mentioned is far greater than what we have mentioned, and the realised Gnostic knows this very well. However, by means of the indicative signs we have mentioned, the seeker can gradually progress towards that which we have omitted from [our] explicit words. In any case, works are only according to intentions; and God knows what lies hidden in His servants' breasts.

THE CAUSES OF THE DREAD OF THOSE WHO HAVE KNOWLEDGE

As for his words in the poem [beginning], 'So know this and act [...]',[1] in this there is a subtle allusion to the denial of absolute knowledge to he who lacks God-fearingness (*taqwā*). God Most High says, *Even so, only those of His servants dread God who have knowledge* (Q.xxxv.28); in other words, amongst His servants, none dread God except those who have knowledge of Him (*al-ʿulamāʾ bihi*), and this is due to their knowledge of His different types of devising and His insouciance were He to destroy the whole world; God Most High says, *Who then shall overrule God in any way if He desires to destroy the Messiah son of Mary, his mother and all those who are on earth*? (Q.v.17). And [this is also] due to their knowledge and appreciation of the wisdom and correctness of wreaking vengeance on the People of Disobedience (*Ahl al-Maʿāṣī*).

God points out by using the expression, 'even so, only' (*innamā*), [in the first Qur'ānic quotation above,] that dread (*khashya*) is negated from anyone other than those who have knowledge and, by extension, that those who have no dread also have no knowledge (*ʿilm*). This is because knowledge is a cause (*sabab*), and a cause

1 This refers to the poem on which the author is here commenting, mentioned at the beginning of this short commentary.

always accompanies that which causes it (*musabbib*). Therefore, dread is of the imperatives of knowledge, which means that knowledge is negated from those who lack dread of God Most High, as a concomitant is negated by the negation of its exigency.

One says for instance, 'Only a person from Baghdad may enter the house', which denies the entry into the house of anyone not from Baghdad. But this does not mean that all those who do not enter are not from Baghdad. Rather, all that this sentence indicates is that being from Baghdad is a cause (*sabab*[an]) of permitting entry into the house. So the person's being from Baghdad is negated by the negation of this permission [to enter], and his being from Baghdad is not a cause of permitting entry into the house to the point where his being from Baghdad is negated by his not entering the house. So understand, for this is a cause of stumbling!

RENUNCIATION AND GOD-FEARINGNESS ARE KEYS TO THE SPIRITUAL PATH

It is clear from the meaning of the Qur'ānic verse mentioned above that the spiritual path (*ṭarīq*) is blocked off from the pouring forth of gnoses (*ʿan inṣibāb al-maʿārif*), which are the knowledges (*ʿulūm*) of existing verities emanating from the Essence of the Necessary Being (*Wājib*) and His Attributes, as well as from all existents—and it is also blocked off from the stations of proximity (*maqāmāt al-qurb*)—which are good character traits and spiritual works—unless it [the spiritual path] is by means of renunciation (*zuhd*) from, and God-fearingness (*taqwā*) regarding: love of this world, reprehensible matters and superfluity, and love of the ego and its attributes. Only then will the spiritual path be opened and will its seeker belong to this group. This is because the slightest disobedience becomes a veil for the heart that prevents it from being pure when remembering God or performing other righteous works. This, in turn, prevents the agreement of the inward aspect with the outward, even if it be in a certain way, and this would amount to hypocrisy on the path of the elect (*ṭarīq al-khawāṣṣ*).

This is because the heart is extremely fine and subtle, like a polished mirror that becomes opaque upon the slightest contact with breath or water. With the limpidity of God-fearingness and perfect renunciation, the heart becomes polished, and the servant gains steadfastness in knowledge. The pinnacle of such knowledge is the servant becoming aware of the intent of the discourse of God Most High in His Glorious Book in terms of endless knowledges, on account of which the wonders of the Qur'ān are immeasurable and its meanings inexhaustible despite its continuous and repeated use.

KNOWLEDGES AND UNDERSTANDINGS OF THE QUR'ĀN

Quoting one of the Predecessors (may God benefit by him) Imam Ghazālī mentioned in his *Revival of the Religious Sciences*[1] (Iḥyā' ᶜulūm al-dīn) that, 'Each verse of the Qur'ān has 60,000 [forms of] understanding (*fahm*), and what remains of their understanding is even greater. This is why understanding the Qur'ān requires that one has knowledge of all of the branches of learning, as well as being privy to the resolves of all created beings, as mentioned by Abū Saᶜīd al-Kharrāz[2] (may God benefit by him).' Ghazālī also quoted another Sufi, who stated that understanding the Qur'ān requires 75,200 different types of knowledge.

Kharrāz did not mean that the person who is steadfast in knowledge should know all of the minutiae of the conventional disciplines; indeed, Abū Bakr and ᶜUmar [b. al-Khaṭṭāb] (may God benefit by them and be well pleased with them) were amongst those steadfast in knowledge, and yet were unsure about the meaning of

1 Ghazālī, *Iḥyā'*, vol. I, p. 23.

2 Abū Saᶜīd Aḥmad b. ᶜĪsā al-Kharrāz, who was one of the greatest masters of Sufism, was from Baghdad. He kept the company of Dhū al-Nūn al-Miṣrī, Sarī Saqaṭī, Bishr b. al-Hārith and others. He wrote several books, including *Kitāb al-Ṣidq*. He died in in the year 286/899. See Ṣafadī, *al-Wāfī bi'l-wafayāt*, vol. VII, p. 275 and Ziriklī, *al-Aᶜlām*, vol. I, p. 191.

the word '*al-abb*' in the words of God Most High, *And dense-tree'd gardens, and fruits, and pastures* (*wa-abbā*), *an enjoyment for you and your flocks* (Q.LXXX.30–32), and thus refrained from engaging in debate about its precise meaning.

In *The Revival of the Religious Sciences*, it was also reported from Ibn Masʿūd (may God be well pleased with father and son) that, on the day that ʿUmar [b. al-Khaṭṭāb] died, he said, 'Nine-tenths of knowledge has vanished today.' Yet, there is no doubt that Abū Bakr was better than he was, nor is there any merit except through genuine knowledge (*wa-lā faḍl illā bi'l-ʿilm al-ḥaqīqī*). What Kharrāz had in mind were genuine universal knowledges (*ʿulūm al-kullīya al-ḥaqīqa*), not the details of the disciplines that are current today, as most of these were not known at all by the vast majority of the Prophetic Companions (*Ṣaḥāba*) or the greatest men from the household of the Prophet (may God bless him and grant him peace). Rather, what was meant was the knowledge of all of the degrees of understanding (*marātib al-fahm*) attained by the different categories of created beings through their aspirations, their focus on God and by cutting themselves off from anything other than Him, as proved by his [Kharrāz's] saying at the end of his remarks, '[...] as well as being privy to the aspirations of all created beings,' which is a valid explanation of the beginning of his sentence, and so it should be understood in this manner.

THE DEGREES OF KNOWLEDGE AND GNOSIS

A servant may be a Knower of God (*ʿālim*[an] *bi'Llāh*) with perfect certitude without being adept at any of the communal obligations (*furūḍ al-kifāyāt*). Those who had knowledge [the scholars] amongst the Prophetic Companions and the greatest men from the Prophet's household (may God benefit by them) were more knowledgeable than the scholars amongst the Followers [of the Predecessors] (*Tābiʿīn*) as far as the verities of certitude and subtle points of gnosis were concerned. And amongst the scholars of the

Followers of the Predecessors were those who had greater knowledge of the discipline of fatwas and legal rulings than some of the Prophetic Companions and members of the Prophetic household, even though there is general agreement that the Prophetic Companions and members of the Prophetic household were better than them. This is only on account of their perfect knowledge of God and certitude in Him. In fact, in terms of the knowledge of fatwas and legal rulings, some of the Prophetic Companions and members of the Prophetic household used to refer people back to the scholars amongst the Followers of the Predecessors, while they themselves taught these same scholars the verities of certitude and subtleties of gnosis because they were more knowledgeable than them in this.

Due to this, the people who possess this knowledge [of the verities of certitude and subtleties of gnosis] are the most honoured of created beings, even if scholars of other disciplines happen to be more devoted to worship than them. As for their exalted merit in knowledge (*ʿilm*), it is because the merit of a person is due to the merit of the knowledge he possess. As for their merit in works (*ʿamal*), it is on account of the fact that the gravity and honour of works are commensurate with the share of knowledge that one has, and the gnostics have exceeded the formal disciplines of knowledge by gaining divinely bestowed forms of knowledge as a result of the pouring forth of the lights of witnessing (*anwār al-mushāhada*) and the eye of certitude (*ʿayn al-yaqīn*). Their knowledge is therefore better than the works of all other scholars, even if the latter toil more than they do.

It was in this context that the Prophetic descendant, the Imām ʿAbd al-Raḥmān al-Saqqāf ʿAlawī remarked, 'A few ounces of the work of the inward aspect (*ʿamal al-bāṭin*) equal three hundred pounds of the work of the outward aspect (*ʿamal al-ẓāhir*).' His sons, Sakrān and Miḥḍār, also mentioned something to the same effect when they said, 'It is due to this that our predecessors from amongst the descendants of ʿAlī (may God benefit by them) have occupied themselves with this well-trodden path and have benefitted mostly from it due to their being enamoured with this exalted method to the point where the Prophetic descendant, Imam ʿAydarūs said, "Were God to bring the dead back to life, they would not counsel the living [to do] anything except what is in *The Revival [of the Religious Sciences]*."' Imām Ghazālī used to say, 'I fear a bad end for whoever does not have a share of knowledge of the inward aspect, the least of which is to believe in it and to submit to its people.'[1]

THE TREMENDOUS WORKS OF THE MASTERS OF HEARTS

Shaykh Abū al-Mawāhib al-Shādhilī[2] used to say, 'I saw the Prophet (may God bless him and grant him peace) in a dream and said to him, "O Messenger of God! I am indeed an intruder on the knowledge of Sufism." He replied, "Read the words of the Folk, for the intruder upon this discipline is indeed the Friend of God. As for the one who has knowledge of it, he is like the star that can never be reached."'

A little of the works of these men is equivalent to a great deal of works from others because they go out of their way to illuminate their work by fulfilling all of its conditions. One unit of prayer performed by them is equivalent to a thousand units of prayer performed by others as indicated by the words of Ibn Masʿūd (may God benefit by him), who said, 'The works performed in one day by some men of this community are heavier upon the scale than the weight of seven heavens and seven earths.'[3]

1 Ghazālī, *Iḥyā'*, vol. I, p. 19.

2 Muḥammad b. Aḥmad Abū al-Mawāhib b. al-Ḥāj al-Tūnisī al-Qāhirī al-Mālikī, better known as Ibn Zaghdān, was born in Tunis in the year 820/1417. He memorised the Qur'ān and several books, and studied with a number of contemporary scholars, such as Ramlī, Birzālī, Mūṣilī and others. He left several books to posterity, including *Marātib al-kamāl* and *Sharḥ al-Ḥikam*. He died in the year 882/1477. See Munāwī, *al-Tabaqāt al-kubrā*, vol. III, pp. 242–252.

3 This was mentioned by Ḥakīm Tirmidhī in *Nawādir al-uṣūl*, and its chain of transmission is not sound (*laysa lahu isnād ṣaḥīḥ*).

And on the authority of Abū Mūsā (may God be well pleased with him it was reported that the Messenger of God (may God bless him and grant him peace) looked at Mount Uhud [a mountain north of Medina] and said, 'Many a man from my community whose utterance of one single letter upon mentioning the formula of God's glorification (*tasbīḥ*) is as heavy as this mountain.'[1] Ḥakīm Tirmidhī[2] commented, 'Thus, one instant for all of the Gnostics brought close [to God] is greater than all of the works that man and jinn perform in as many years as the Prophet Nūḥ (peace be upon him) lived.'

Abū al-Qāsim al-Ṣiqillī said, 'One unit of prayer from a gnostic (*ʿārif*) is better than a thousand units of prayer from a scholar (*ʿālim*); and one single breath from one of the People of the Reality of Divine Oneness (*Ahl Ḥaqīqat al-Tawḥīd*) is better than the works of each gnostic and scholar.' It was also mentioned in *The Revival [of the Religious Sciences]* by Ghazālī that, 'One single breath from a Gnostic is better than the rank of a thousand martyrs.' It is for this reason that the Gnostics said that one single breath of the Pole, the Prophetic descendant our grandfather al-Faqīh al-Muqaddam Muḥammad b. ʿAlī ʿAlawī (may God benefit by him) was equivalent to the works of all mankind and jinn. How could it be otherwise when it was he who said, 'Amongst the Friends of God, I am like the Prophet Muḥammad (may God bless him and grant him peace) was amongst the prophets.' In fact, even though some of these Gnostics do not perform a great many supererogatory acts of worship, they are still better than the scholars who perform these a great deal, due to the saying of the Prophet (may God bless him and grant him peace), 'The

1 This saying was also mentioned by Ḥakīm Tirmidhī in *Nawādir al-uṣūl*, but it does not have an authentic chain of transmission (*laysa lahu isnād thābit*).

2 Dhahabī wrote a biography of him in his work, *Tadhkirat al-ḥuffāẓ*. He wrote, 'Ḥakīm Tirmidhī, Imam Abū ʿAbd Allāh Muḥammad b. ʿAlī b. al-Ḥasan b. Bishr, the Ascetic, the Ḥāfiẓ, the Muezzin, Master of Literary Works. He transmitted traditions from his father and from Qutayba b. Saʿīd, al-Ḥasan b. ʿUmar b. Shaqīq, Ṣāliḥ b. ʿAbd Allāh al-Tirmidhī, Yaḥyā ibn Mūsā, ʿUtba b. ʿAbd Allāh al-Marwazī, ʿUbbād b. Yaʿqūb al-Rawājinī [...].' He died in the year 320/932.

merit of the man of knowledge over the devotee is like my merit over my community.'[1] Now, there is no relationship between his merit and that of his community unless it be like the relationship between being and nothingness; but the merit of the man of knowledge is compared to the Prophet's merit (may God bless him and grant him peace) over his community because he is the locus of the Divine Glance (*maḥall al-Naẓar al-Ilāhī*) and an intermediary of His emanation (*wāsiṭat fayḍihi*) just as the Prophet was, except the Prophet (may God bless him and grant him peace) had this directly, whereas the man of knowledge has it indirectly through his emulation of the Prophet (may God bless him and grant him peace).

THE PREFERENCE FOR THE KNOWLEDGE OF GOD OVER MERE KNOWLEDGE

If you said that the aforementioned Prophetic saying is proof that this knowledge is not conclusive because—in absolute terms—both the man of knowledge and the devotee fall under it, then this is true for both the formal man of knowledge and the devotee with no knowledge (which is what appears to be understood from the saying).

Then my answer to this would be what I have [already] mentioned in relation to the Prophetic Companions. [They] used to refer people to some of the scholars amongst the Followers for answers to their legal questions because [those scholars] were more knowledgeable than [the Companions] in this field; although [the Companions] did teach this knowledge to those very scholars. If the aforementioned Prophetic saying did not allude to this knowledge, then it necessarily follows that some of the scholars amongst the Followers were preferred over some of the scholars amongst the Prophetic Companions; yet no one has ever claimed this.

1 Narrated by Tirmidhī, '*Bāb mā jā'a fī faḍl al-fiqh ʿalā al-ʿibāda*', *Sunan al-Tirmidhī*, *Kitāb al-ʿilm*, no. 2685. Tirmidhī stated that this saying was well authenticated (*ḥasan*)/uncommon (*gharīb*)/rigorously authenticated (*ṣaḥīḥ*).

In sum, this knowledge is like the cream extracted from milk in relation to formal knowledge; milk here being the knowledge of the formal scholars who specialise in the theoretical basis of faith and certitude. It is undoubtedly true that the formal man of knowledge has merit over the ignorant devotee due to the knowledge that he possesses, just as the person who has this knowledge has merit over both the formal man of knowledge and the devotee because of the knowledge he possesses. Moreover, the term, 'devotee' (*ʿābid*), applies both to the man of knowledge who has this knowledge, and to the man of formal knowledge.

Amongst the proofs of the merit of this knowledge with which the Gnostics (may God benefit by them) have preoccupied themselves, is the saying of the unique Pole Ismāʿīl al-Jabartī al-Hāshimī al-ʿUqayli[1] (may God benefit by him), 'A man may obtain through one point of this knowledge of ours what he will not obtain through fifty years of spiritual struggle.' Another proof of the nobility of this knowledge is the saying of the master of the Sufis, Junayd (may God benefit by him), 'Believing in this path of ours is itself sainthood', meaning a share of it, even if this is inferior; and the person who has this belief does not come under the category of the Friends of God, just as the person who believes in prophethood has a share of it, even though prophethood is not ascribed to him.

Another proof of the nobility of this knowledge is the saying of Zarrūq[2] (may God benefit by him), 'Perfect well-being is the quietude of the heart (*sukūn al-qalb*) towards God through certitude, which entails contentment and utter submission (*li'l-riḍā wa'l-taslīm*). All

1 Ismā'īl b. Ibrāhīm b. ʿAbd al-Ṣamad al-Jabartī, the Gnostic and spiritual master, was born in Zabid. No Sufi master in Yemen had more students and followers than him. He died in the year 875/1470. See Aḥmad b. Aḥmad b. ʿAbd al-Laṭīf al-Zabīdī, *Ṭabaqāt al-khawāṣṣ ahl al-ṣidq wa'l-ikhlāṣ*, Cairo: al-Maṭbaʿa al-Maymaniyya, [no date], pp. 37–40 and Munāwī, *al-Tabaqāt al-kubrā*, vol. III, p. 172.

2 Shaykh Aḥmad b. Muḥammad b. ʿĪsā al-Burnusī al-Fāsī al-Mālikī was born in Fez in the year 846/1442. He is the author of numerous books. He died in 899/1493. See Munāwī, *al-Tabaqāt al-kubrā*, vol. III, pp. 166–172 and Sakhāwī, *al-Ḍaw' al-lāmiʿ*, vol. I, p. 222.

misfortune lies in doubt, confusion and wavering between swarming thoughts, as the person who is in this state will never find peace, nor settle his mind on anything.'

Another proof of the nobility of this knowledge is a report that mentions that a man went to see Muʿādh [b. Jabal] (may God be well pleased with him) and asked him, 'Tell me about two men: one of whom exerts the utmost effort in acts of worship, he performs many works and has very few sins, but his certitude (*yaqīn*) is weak because he sometimes has doubts (*shakk*).' Muʿādh replied, 'His doubts will thwart his works.' The man then said, 'Tell me then about a [second] man who performs few works, but his certitude is strong and his sins are many.' Muʿādh did not answer, so the man said, 'By God! If the doubts of the first man have thwarted his good works, the certitude of this second man will efface all of his sins.' Upon this, Muʿādh took the man by his hand and said, 'I have not seen anyone who has more understanding [of religion] (*afqah*) than this.'

It was also mentioned in the counsels of Luqmān (peace be upon him) to his son, 'O dear son! One cannot perform works without certitude; and no man works except in proportion to his certitude, and no performer of works slackens in them unless his certitude has diminished.'

In sum, works are of no benefit without the luminosity (*tanwīr*) that benefits one in relation to God's with-ness (*li'l-maʿiyya*), and which expands one's breast (*ṣadr*), as Muʿādh has said. In fact, this luminosity removes the darkness of the acts of disobedience that makes it easy for one to turn [towards God] in repentance, as mentioned by the man who questioned Muʿādh. There can be no work without this luminosity; and that is because a work is not so called until it fulfils all of the rights (*ḥuqūqihi*) that are associated with it. This, however, cannot happen while the darkness of the ego remains, as pointed out by Luqmān (peace be upon him).

So pay attention, O desirous seeker, for the Gnostics have said, 'When God wishes evil upon a servant, He closes the door of works in his face, and opens the door of laziness for him [instead].' They also said, 'The sign that God is well pleased with a servant is that he is enlivened upon performing acts of obedience and lazy upon engaging in disobedience; whereas the sign of His displeasure with him is that [the servant] is enlivened upon engaging in disobedience and lazy upon performing acts of obedience.'

THE MERIT OF SPIRITUAL STRUGGLES

It is for this reason that the Pole, the Prophetic descendant ʿAbd Allāh al-ʿAydarūs said, 'All of the treasures [lie] in the buried treasures of spiritual struggles.' And he quoted the following verse of poetry: 'Decisions are commensurate with the People of Determination, / And noble character traits are commensurate with the People of Nobility.'

The brother of ʿAydarūs, the Prophetic descendant, the Pole ʿAlī b. Abī Bakr said, 'Through earnestness (*jidd*) and striving (*ijtihād*) the utmost goal is reached, and through sound resolve the lamp of God-given success shines forth. Wishes never come true through slackness, nor will he who lies down on the couch of laziness ever obtain his hope. And beware of saying, "If something is predestined, then it will surely come to pass, and if it has been preordained, then it will definitely take place", for it is through action that blessings happen, and it is through shaking [trees] that fruits fall [to the ground]. Indeed, the infertile mother will always remain sterile.' Then he quoted the following lines of poetry:

> In proportion with earnestness, noble things are acquired,
> And whoever desires sublimity must forgo sleep at night;
> You aspire to glory, yet sleep at night,
> Whoever seeks pearls must surely dive into the sea;
> Whoever aspires to sublimity without toil,
> Wastes his life in seeking the impossible.

It was reported in a saying that, 'When God desires good for a servant, He appoints an admonisher (*wāʿiẓ*^{an}) within him who commands him and warns him.'[1] In this context, one poet said: 'The ego is not warned against its error / If it does not have a curb to check it from within.'

THE BINDING OF CAUSES TO EFFECTS

You should also know that Divine Power (*Qudra*) flows through causes and effects together: [that is,] through the action of the cause (*musabbib*), and through the action of the effect (*musabbab*). Divine Power subsists in causes and effects even though it can do without both, but Divine Wisdom (*Ḥikma*) has decreed that causes are bound to their effects because this is the predominant manifestation of Divine Power in this worldly abode. This is why it has been decreed that causes are bound to their effects in this world, just as in the Afterlife; it is Divine Power that will be manifested, while causes and effects will be latent.

Moreover, works in the Afterlife will be in accordance with how you exited from this world to the next. Therefore, whoever has been granted success in seeking causes in this world, this is a sign that one will acquire their effects in terms of what God the Magnificent has promised, just as smoke is an indication of fire. And it also be that such good fortune with Divine Oneness may occur without this. However, just as sustenance (*rizq*) is only acquired through action, although categorically believing that Divine Power can provide it to the servant without action, so too can abundant sustenance come one's way without any action. This is why good fortune is connected to works on the whole.

1 Narrated by Aḥmad b. Ḥanbal in *Kitāb al-zuhd* as the words of Ibn Sīrīn, and it is of the soundest opinion (*huwa al-ṣawāb*); see Ibn Ḥanbal, *Kitāb al-Zuhd*, ed. Muḥammad al-Saʿīd b. Basyūnī Zaghlūl, Beirut: Dār al-Kitāb al-ʿArabī, 1414/1993, p. 306. It was also narrated by Daylamī in *Musnad al-Firdaws*, also from Ibn Sīrīn from Umm Salama (may God be well pleased with her), who attributed it to the Prophet (may God bless him and grant him peace). However, the saying is not sound (*lā yathbut*).

THE CATEGORIES OF GOD'S ACTIONS

To clarify what we have mentioned above, know that God's Actions (*Afʿāl Allāh*) are of two types. One type unfolds through the setting into order (*tadbīr*) of causes and effects (*ḥikma*); in other words, things unfolding in the span of a limited period of time, just as planted trees, take time to yield fruits. The other type unfolds through the disposal (*taṣrīf*) of His Power (*Qudra*), such as His saying to a thing, 'Be!' and it instantly is. Those amongst the Friends of God Most High to whom pure gnosis has been revealed see the disposal of Divine Power from the secret of the setting into order of causes and effects. That is to say, He Who is able to sustain the body by means of physical food is also able to sustain it through food from the All-Merciful without any apparent sustenance, as my master Abū ʿAbd Allāh al-Qurashī[1] (may God benefit by him) said, 'The Gnostic is the one who deems the disposal of Divine Power, and the setting into order of causes and effects, to be equal in his eyes.' This is because the Gnostic who has reached the station of the disposal of Divine Power (*maqām taṣrīf al-Qudra*)—by which I mean, if he says to a thing, 'Be!' and it is in a single instant, like a tree giving fruits in an instant (unlike how fruits grow normally)—and then does something that conforms to the setting into order of causes and effects (*tadbīr al-ḥikma*)— such as planting a tree and the tree then yielding fruits in due course—does not differentiate between the two of them. If he finds the slightest difference between these two actions by being amazed by one of them, or that these two actions are not equal in his eyes, then he is not a Gnostic.

If that is not the case, then God can do without causes (*asbāb*); in fact, causes do not have any effect (*athar*) as the real Agent (*Mu'aththir*) is God Most High at [the time of] their coming into existence (*ʿinda wujūdihā*); [any effect is] not by means of them (*lā bihā*). Nonetheless,

1 Muḥammad b. Aḥmad b. Ibrāhīm, Abū ʿAbd Allāh al-Qurashī was an eminent Gnostic and a noble Sufi. He was originally from Algeciras in al-Andalus. He lived in Egypt and then moved to Jerusalem where he died in 599/1202. See Munāwī, *al-Tabaqāt al-kubrā*, vol. II, pp. 283–287.

God's unceasing *Sunna* (that is, His Custom) comes to pass. [And] in [God's] giving causes their right (*ḥaqquhā*) to determine the assigning of causality to the manifestation of subtleties and marvels of knowledge in their arrangement, [His *Sunna*] does not act against [those causes]—unless a prophetic or saintly miracle (*muʿjiza aw karāma*) is manifested. [Meaning: God's *Sunna* does not contradict the subtle rules of causality unless a miracle occurs, which—by definition—entails breaking the rules of causality.]

Thus, out of concern for a servant, God may open a door of infliction of misfortune for him, in which God shows him His complete subjugation of sinners, so that He immediately punishes him for each [act of] disobedience that he commits, in contrast to the person who is lured to perdition and is so ignorant that he imagines that he has been granted respite. This immediate punishment applies to even the smallest sin, such as committing an impropriety relating to the spiritual path, or to what is considered a sin by the Sacred Law, which is the absolute sin in the eyes of the People of the Outward [Disciplines of the Sacred Law] (*Ahl al-Ẓāhir*) and the People of the Spiritual Path and Ultimate Reality (*Ahl al-Ṭarīqa wa'l-Ḥaqīqa*). He will immediately incur a punishment if he commits something like this; and if not immediately, then in the course of that day or the following night. His punishment will never be delayed by more than that, and he will know it. One Sufi (may God benefit by him) said, 'I recognise that I have committed a sin from the bad manners that my servant boy shows towards me; God disciplines me as a consequence of what has proceeded from me. This [comes] from the care (*ʿināya*) of God Most High for His servant; may God grant us this and encompass us with His care.'

THE NECESSITY OF PRACTISING ONE'S KNOWLEDGE

You should also know that it was reported that the Messenger of God (may God bless him and grant him peace) said, 'Satan may outstrip you in knowledge.' So he was asked, 'How will he outstrip us in knowledge?' He replied, 'He will say, "Seek knowledge and do not practise it until you truly know," so the servant will continue to seek knowledge and postpone works until he dies without having performed any works.'[1]

It is for this reason that one of my teachers (may God have mercy on him) used to say, 'He who pursues knowledge but does not practise what he learns is like someone who constantly performs the minor ritual ablution but does not offer a single unit of prayer.' He also often said to one of his students in allusion to practising one's knowledge, 'Perform the minor ritual ablution and then pray;' in other words, just as you have learned beneficial knowledge, so then practise it. Otherwise, as one poet (may God have mercy on him) has said: 'If knowledge without God-fearingness were an honour, / Satan would have been one of God's outstanding created beings.'

THE LIGHT OF THE KNOWLEDGE OF GOD MOST HIGH

In this context, Ibn Masᶜūd (may God be well pleased with him) said, 'Knowledge is not about how many reports one transmits, but rather about how much dread (*khashya*) of God one has'; in other words, the goal of knowledge is practice, which is instigated by the dread of God that accompanies knowledge.

As for the words of the author in his short poem, '[...] a pitch-black night will be dissipated',[2] it will be dissipated by means of the bright day of the knowledge of God Most High, which, despite its complete manifestation in created beings, is veiled from them due to His Essential Independence (*bi-ṣifat Ghanāhu al-Dhātī*), and He Himself is veiled from them by being far transcendent above

1 Narrated by Khaṭīb Baghdādī in *al-Jāmiᶜ li-akhlāq al-rāwī wa-ādāb al-sāmiᶜ* from Anas, who attributed to the Prophet (may God bless him and grant him peace); and its chain of transmission is weak (*ḍaᶜīf*).

2 This extract is from the author's poem, which is found at the beginning of the present work and which is the subject of this commentary.

the attributes of created beings. And because something cannot apprehend that which is not in it, [so too] do created beings not apprehend Him; so by necessity, He is veiled from them, and He is also veiled from them through His subjugation of the objects of created beings' perception, lest they reach Him.

Nonetheless, complete manifestation (*kamāl al-ẓuhūr*) does not contradict veiling (*iḥtijāb*), as is the case with the sun in relation to bats. In fact, total manifestation may require veiling, for the light of the sun is so bright that some people confuse it with the colours of things. If it were not for the differentiation of light and colour at the onset of sunset, the confusion that the light of the sun is nothing but the colours of things would persist. However, when the sun sets, the colours of things disappear, and one realises that the light of the sun is one thing while the colours of things are something different.

This, however, is not the case with regards to the existence of God Most High, for His Radiance (*Ishrāqahu*) over all is indiscriminate in the first place, and so the confusion remains. So Glory be to Him Who is the First and the Last, the Outwardly Manifest and the Inwardly Hidden, the kernel of the verities of Whose Names and Attributes—let alone the kernel of His Absolute Essence—is not apprehended by the state of insight (in other words, the power of the spirit). And if this is the state of insight (*baṣīra*), what would one say about the state of physical sight (*baṣar*) or reason (*ᶜaql*)?

It is for this reason that the most veracious one (may God be well pleased with him) said, 'The inability to grasp complete perception is [itself] a perception.' He also said, 'Glory be to He Who there is no way of knowing other than by being unable to truly know Him.' This is because He is the Majestic, the Mighty, the All-Conquering, the Vast, the All-Knowing; The One Whose Reality no one knows except Him. The Gnostic Ismāᶜīl al-Jabartī (may God benefit by him) said, 'The Qur'ān contains all of the Names of God Most High by which He is known, and those by which He is not known. His name, 'God' (*Allāh*), combines all of the degrees of the names, and the names by which He is known, such as the Sacred Law (*Sharīʿa*) and the Essence of God (glorified and exalted is He), have made the Qur'ān inimitable.'

He also said, 'God is the Greatest! The Names of God have proved incapable of knowing God; the Names of God seek Him just as we do.' His student, the Gnostic Aḥmad al-Raddād[1] (may God benefit by him) said, 'This means that the names qua names seek the very essence of the named, and so the names only signify those meanings that they support. As for the names, insofar as they are that which is named itself (*al-musammā iyyāhu*) and its essence, they are one substance that encompasses every substance and vestige; and yet there is no substance and no vestige, no knowledge and no information to convey. And God surrounds all things.'

Glory be to He Who, due to His intense Manifestation, is veiled from us by His Light, so that we may only know Him in certain respects. In sum, He is uniquely distinct from the loci of manifestation due to the implication of, 'God was, and nothing besides Him was with Him';[2] and He is also manifested in them due to the implication of His words, *He is with you wherever you are* (Q.LVII.4). However, God is not restricted by this due to the implication of His words, *Does He not encompass everything*? (Q.XLI.54).

And May God's blessings and peace be upon the greatest means of intercession with Him (*al-wasīla al-kubrā ilayhi*), and upon his household and his Companions, who successfully obtained a great share from what he had.

1 He was Aḥmad b. al-Qāḍī Riḍā al-Dīn Abī Bakr b. Muḥammad al-Raddād al-Bakrī al-Taymī al-Qurashī al-Yamanī. The Sufi leadership in Yemen ultimately reached him. He went to Mecca for the Pilgrimage and he was the author of many works, including *Reasons for Mercy and Intentions for Forgiveness* (*Mūjibāt al-raḥma wa-ʿazā'im al-maghfira*). He died in the year 821/1418. See Munāwī, *al-Tabaqāt al-kubrā*, vol. III, pp. 157–159 and Zabīdī, *Ṭabaqāt al-khawāṣṣ*, pp. 30–32.

2 Narrated by Bukhārī (no. 3191) on the authority of ʿImrān b. Ḥusayn; see '*Bāb mā jā'a fī qawlihi taʿālā "Alladhī yabda'ū al-khalq thumma yuʿīduh"*', in *Ṣaḥīḥ al-Bukhārī*, *Kitāb bad' al-khalq*, no. 3191.

Here ends this short commentary that we have derived from the works, *The Knowledge of the Gnostics* (ʿAwārif al-ʿārifīn), and *The Flowing Tears of the Subtleties of those who have Reached God* (Dhawārif laṭā'if al-wāṣilīn) and, especially, *The Gifts of Knowledge* (ʿAwārif al-maʿārif)[1] and its commentary, *Additional Subtleties* (Zawārif al-laṭā'if), by Shaykh ʿAlī al-Mahā'imī[2] (may God be well pleased with all and benefit by them at every instant and moment).

And may God's blessings and peace be upon Muḥammad, and upon his household and Companions. Amen. Praise be to God, Lord of all the Worlds! He is sufficient for us; what an excellent Guardian is He! There is no might or power save through God, the Transcendent, the Mighty. What an excellent Protector and Helper is He!

1 By Shaykh Shihāb al-Dīn, Abū Ḥafṣ ʿUmar b. Muḥammad al-Suhrawardī, who died in 586/1190. See Ibn Kathīr, *al-Bidāya wa'l-nihāya*, Beirut: Dār al-Fikr, 1987, vol. XIII, pp. 138–139.

2 Shaykh ʿAlī b. Aḥmad b. Ibrāhīm b. Ismā'īl al-Dakanī al-Hindī al-Ḥanafī, better known as Makhdūm Mahā'imī (Mahā'im being an area in the Deccan in India). He was a jurisprudent and a Sufi who wrote several publications, including the commentary mentioned here. See Ziriklī, *al-Aʿlām*, vol. IV, p. 257 and Ṣiddīq Ḥasan Khān, *Abjad al-ʿulūm*.

BIBLIOGRAPHY

Abū Yaʿlā, Aḥmad b. ʿAlī b. al-Muthannā, *Musnad Abū Yaʿlā*, ed. Muṣṭafā ʿAbd al-Qādir ʿAtā, Beirut: Dār al-Kutub al-ʿIlmiyya, 1998.

Akkach, Samer, *The Letters of a Sufi Scholar: The Correspondence of ʿAbd al-Ghanī al-Nābulusī (1641–1731)*, Leiden: Brill, 2010.

ʿAydarūs, ʿAbd al-Raḥmān b. Muṣṭafā b. Shaykh al-, *al-ʿArf al-ʿāṭir fī maʿrifat al-khawāṭir wa-ghayrihā min al-jawāhir*, Amman: Royal Aal Al-Bayt Institute for Islamic Thought, [no date].

ʿAydarūs, ʿAbd al-Qādir b. Shaykh b. ʿAbd Allāh al-, *al-Nūr al-sāfir ʿan akhbār al-qarn al-ʿāshir*, ed. Aḥmad Ḥālū et. al., Beirut: Dār Ṣādir, 2001.

Bābānī, Ismāʿīl b. Muḥammad b. Amīn al-Baghdādī al-, *Hadiyyat al-ʿārifīn*, Beirut: Dār al-Fikr, 1982.

Bang, Anne, *Sufis and Scholars of the Sea: Family Networks in East Africa, 1860–1925*, London: Routledge, 2003.

Bukhārī, Muḥammad b. Ismāʿīl al-, *Ṣaḥīḥ al-Bukhārī bi-ḥāshiyat al-Imām al-Sindī*, Mecca: Maktabat ʿAbbās Aḥmad al-Bāz, [no date].

Dhahabī, Muḥammad b. Aḥmad b. ʿUthmān, al-, *Siyar aʿlām al-nubalā'*, ed. Shuʿayb al-Arna'ūt et. al., Beirut: Mu'asasat al-Risāla, 1985.

Ghazālī, Abū Ḥāmid Muḥammad al-, *Iḥyā' ʿulūm al-dīn*, Beirut: Dār al-Maʿrifa, [no date].

———, *Iḥyā' ʿulūm al-dīn*, Book XXI: *Kitāb sharḥ ʿajā'ib al-qalb*, trans. Walter J. Skellie as *The Marvels of the Heart*, Louisville, KY: Fons Vitae, 2010.

Ḥabshī, ʿAydarūs b. ʿUmar b. ʿAydarūs al-, *ʿIqd al-yawāqīt al-jawhariyya wa-simṭ al-ʿayn al-dhahabiyya bi-dhikr ṭarīq al-sādāt al-ʿalawiyya*, Cairo: al-Maṭbaʿa al-ʿĀmiriyya al-Sharafiyya, 1317/1899.

Ḥākim, Abū ʿAbd Allāh al-Naysābūrī al-, *al-Mustadrak ʿalā al-ṣaḥiḥayn wa-bi-dhaylihi talkhīṣ al-mustadrak li'l-Dhahabī*, Riyadh: Maktabat al-Maʿārif, [no date].

Haythamī, ʿAlī b. Abī Bakr al-, *Majmaʿ al-zawā'id wa-manbaʿ al-fawā'id*, Beirut: Mu'assasat al-Maʿārif, 1986.

Ibn ʿArabī, Muḥyī al-Dīn Muḥammad b. ʿAlī, *al-Futūḥāt al-makkiyya*, Dār Ṣādir, [no date].

Ibn ʿAṭāʾ Allāh al-Iskandarī, Tāj al-Dīn Aḥmad, *Laṭāʾif al-minan fī manāqib al-shaykh Abī al-ʿAbbās al-Mursī wa-shaykhihi al-Shādhilī Abī Ḥasan*, ed. ʿAbd al-Ḥalīm Maḥmūd. Cairo: Maṭbaʿat al-Iḥsān, [no date].

———, *Miftāḥ al-falāḥ wa-miṣbāḥ al-arwāḥ fī dhikr Allāh al-Karīm al-Fattāḥ*, ed. Muḥammad Ibrāhīm, Beirut: Dār al-Kutub al-ʿIlmiyya, [no date].

Ibn Ḥajar al-ʿAsqalānī, Aḥmad, *Fatḥ al-Bārī bi-sharḥ Ṣaḥīḥ al-Bukhārī*, Beirut: Dār Ṣādir, [no date].

Ibn Ḥanbal, Aḥmad, *Kitāb al-zuhd*, ed. Muḥammad al-Saʿīd b. Basyūnī Zaghlūl, Beirut: Dār al-Kitāb al-ʿArabī, 1414/1993.

Ibn Ḥibbān, Abū Ḥātim Muḥammad b. Hibbān al-Bustī, *al-Iḥsān bi-tartīb Ṣaḥiḥ Ibn Ḥibbān*, ed. Kamāl Yūsuf al-Ḥūt, Beirut: Dār al-Kutub al-ʿIlmiyya, 1987.

Ibn al-ʿImād, ʿAbd al-Ḥayy b. Aḥmad Abū al-Falāḥ, *Shadharāt al-dhahab fī akhbār man dhahab*, ed. ʿAlī Maḥmūd al-Arnaʾūt, Damascus: Dār Ibn Kathīr, 1986–1995.

Ibn al-Jawzī, Abū al-Faraj Jamāl al-Din, *Ṣifat al-ṣafwa*, ed. Mahmūd Fākhūrī and Muḥammad Rawās Qalʿajī, Beirut: Dār al-Maʿrifa, 1979.

Ibn Khallikān, Aḥmad b. Muḥammad, *Wafayāt al-aʿyān wa-anbāʾ abnāʾ al-zamān*, ed. Iḥsān ʿAbbās, Beirut: Dār al-Thaqāfa, [no date].

Ibn Kathīr, Ismāʿīl b. ʿUmar al-Qurashī, *al-Bidāya wa'l-nihāya*, Beirut: Dār al-Fikr, 1987.

Jabartī, ʿAbd al-Raḥmān b. Ḥasan al-, *ʿAjāʾib al-āthār fī al-tarājim wa'l-akhbār aw Taʾrīkh al-Jabartī*, Cairo: al-Maṭbaʿa al-ʿĀmiriyya al-Sharafiyya, 1322/1904.

Kaḥḥāla, ʿUmar Riḍā al-, *Muʿjam al-muʾallifīn: Tarājim muṣannifī al-kutub al-ʿarabiyya*, Beirut: Dār Iḥyāʾ al-Turāth al-ʿArabī, [no date].

Kattānī, ʿAbd al-Ḥayy b. ʿAbd al-Kabīr, ʿAbd al-Kabīr al-, *Fihris al-fahāris wa'l-athbāt wa-muʿjam al-maʿājim wa'l-mashyakhāt wa'l-musalsalāt*, ed. Iḥsān ʿAbbās, Beirut: Dār al-Gharb al-Islāmī, [no date].

Kramers, J. H., et al., *Encyclopaedia of Islam*, 11 vols., new edn., Leiden: E. J. Brill, 1954–2002.

Munāwī, Zayn al-Dīn Muḥammad, *al-Ṭabaqāt al-kubrā aw al-Kawākib al-duriyya fī tarājim al-sāda al-ṣūfiyya*, ed. Muḥammad Adīb Jādir, Beirut: Dār Ṣādir, 1999.

Murādī, Muḥammad Khalīl b. ʿAlī al-, *Silk al-durar fī aʿyān al-qarn al-thānī ʿashar*, Beirut: Dār al-Bashāʾir/Dār Ibn Ḥazm, 1988.

Muslim, Muslim b. al-Ḥajjāj al-Qushayrī, *Ṣaḥīḥ Muslim*, ed. Muḥammad Fuʾād ʿAbd al-Bāqī, Cairo: Dār Iḥyāʾ al-Kutub al-ʿArabiyya, 1955.

Peskes, Esther, *al-Aidarus und seine Erben*, Stuttgart: Franz Steiner Verlag, 2005.

Qāri', ʿAlī al-Harawī al-Makkī al-, *al-Maṣnūʿ fī maʿrifat al-ḥādīth al-mawḍūʿ*, ed. ʿAbd al-Fattāḥ Abū Ghudda, Aleppo: al-Maṭbūʿāt al-Islamiyya, 1994.

Ṣafadī, Khalīl b. Aybak b. ʿAbd Allāh al-, *al-Wāfī bi'l-wafayāt*, ed. Helmut Ritter et. al., Wiesbaden: Franz Steiner, 1983–2005.

Sakhāwī, Muḥammad b. ʿAbd al-Raḥmān al-, *al-Maqāsid al-ḥasana fī bayān kathīr min al-aḥādīth al-mushtahara ʿalā al-alsina*, ed. Muḥammad ʿUthmān al-Khisht, Beirut: Dār al-Kitab al-ʿArabī, 1985.

———, *al-Ḍaw' al-lāmiʿ li-ahl al-qarn al-tāsiʿ*, Beirut: Dār Maktabat al-Ḥayāt, [no date].

Shaʿrānī, ʿAbd al-Wahhāb al-, *al-Ṭabaqāt al-kubrā*, Cairo: Maktabat Muṣṭafā al-Bābī al-Ḥalabī, 1954.

Shāṭirī, Muḥammad b. Aḥmad al-, *Adwār ta'rīkh al-ḥaḍramī*, Medina: Dār al-Muhājir, 1392/1972.

Shillī, Muḥammad b. Abī Bakr Bā ʿAlawī al-, *al-Mashraʿ al-rawī fī manāqib al-sāda al-kirām Āl Abī ʿAlawī*, Cairo: al-Maṭbaʿa al-ʿĀmiriyya al-Sharafiyya, 1319/1901.

Tirmidhī, Muḥammad b. ʿĪsā al-, *Sunan al-Tirmidhī*, ed. Ibrāhīm ʿAṭwa ʿAwwaḍ, Cairo: Dār al-Ḥadīth, [no date].

Zabīdī, Aḥmad b. ʿAbd al-Laṭīf al-Sharjī al-, *Ṭabaqāt al-khawāṣṣ ahl al-ṣidq wa'l-ikhlāṣ*, Cairo: al-Maṭbaʿa al-Muyammaniyya, [no date].

Zabīdī, Muḥammad b. Muḥammad al-Ḥusaynī Murtaḍā al-, *Itḥāf al-sāda al-mutaqqīn bi-sharḥ Iḥyā'* ʿulūm *al-dīn*, Cairo: al-Maṭbaʿa al-Muyammaniyya, 1311/1894.

Ziriklī, Khayr al-Dīn al-, *al-Aʿlām: Qāmūs tarājim li-ashhar al-rijāl wa'l-nisā' min al-ʿarab wa'l-mustaʿribīn wa'l-mustashriqīn*, Beirut: Dār al-ʿIlm li'l-Malāyīn, 1984.

INDEX

Divine Oneness (*tawḥīd*), 5, 19, 59, 75, 89, 115, 132; light of Divine Oneness, 19; the One/*Wāḥid*, 117; see also God
doubts (*shakk*), 130

ecstasy (*wajd*), 89–91; commotions ensued by, 89; complete absence, 90; complete compulsion, 89
ego (*nafs*), 3; character traits, 7, 8, 15, 56, 78; claim of extinction and subsistence, 11, 51; confusion of what is beneficial with what is harmful, 7, 9, 30, 33; darkness of, 8, 49, 130; essential evil of, 10; extinction of, 59; greatest defects of, 11; as the greatest enemy, 13–14; heart/ego confusion, 23–4; human capability, 30; imaginal forms produced by, 109; languor strengthens the ego, 102, 103; love of, 16, 122; obfuscations of, 20–2; the Perfected ones and the defects of the ego, 11–13; rising up and cloaking of itself, 11; struggle against, 13–16, 25; turbidity of, 63, 74, 78, 92; a veil between the servant and his Lord, 16, 66; see also base desire; ego as source of motivating thoughts; soul
ego as source of motivating thoughts (*khāṭir al-nafs*), xii–xiii, 1, 5, 7, 8, 24, 27, 28, 29; base desire, 20, 23, 28, 32; *khāṭir al-nafs*/*khāṭir al-shayṭān* distinction, 16–17; rejecting egotistic motivating thoughts, 19; see also ego; motivating thoughts, sources of
Esotericists (*Bāṭiniyya*), 3
expansiveness, 23; expansion of the heart, 58–9, 64, 130
extinction (*fanā'*), 41, 117–18; disclosure by essence, 117; ego's claim of extinction, 11, 51; extinction in the Divine Essence, 119; extinction of the ego, 92; extinction of the heart, 51–2; extinction of the will, 117; inward extinction, 117–18; outward extinction, 117; solitude and retreat, 92; state of extinction, 80; station of extinction, 28, 118–21 (in the Divine Attributes, 118–19; in the Divine Essence, 119)

faith (*īmān*): faith in Divine Power, 42; rejecting egotistic motivating thoughts by means of faith, 19
fanā', see extinction
al-Faqīh al-Muqaddam, Muḥammad b. ʿAlī b. ʿAlawī, x, xi, 42–3, 127
fasting, 38, 40–1, 44, 46, 73; reasons for not being harmed by hunger, 38–9; secret of the power of continual fasting, 42–3
fear (*khawf*), 15, 27, 38, 89
fitna, see sedition
fiṭra, see primordial nature
Followers of the Predecessors (*Tābiʿūn*), 5n, 124–5, 128
The Fragrant Scent, ix, xii–xiv; *Ḥadīth*, xiii; poem, 1; Qur'ān, xiii; Sufi authorities referred to in, xi; translation of, xii, xiv; see also al-ʿAydarūs, ʿAbd al-Raḥmān b. Muṣṭafā
Friends of God (*awliyā' Allāh*), 42, 44, 73, 90, 119, 126, 127, 129, 133
fujūr, see debauchery

al-Ghazālī, Abū Ḥāmid Muḥammad, xi, 52, 86, 108, 113–14; languor, 103–104; motivating thoughts, xiin; Qur'ān, 123; *Revival of the Religious Sciences*, 15n, 123, 124, 126, 127

gnosis (*maʿrifa*), 6, 46; degrees of knowledge and gnosis, 124–6; divine knowledge, 17; heart as locus of, 47; knowledge of the heart, 23; knowledge of the soul, 9–10, 23; light of gnosis, 19; perfect gnosis, 10; preference for the knowledge of God over mere knowledge, 128–31; rank of, 3; Realised Gnostic, 69; see also gnostic

gnostic (*ʿārif*): merit of the man of knowledge over the devotee and the scholar, 127–8, 129; prayer from, 127; states of the gnostics, 83–6; station of the Disposal of Power and the setting into order of causes and effects, 133; see also gnosis

God, 136–7; Attributes, 54, 108, 136; beholding the Divine, 78, 80, 105, 108, 112; Character Traits of God, 119; Divine attraction, 53–4, 70; Divine Care, 114, 134; Divine Essence, 49, 54, 77, 118, 119, 136, 137; Divine Essential Independence, 135; Divine Love, absorption in, 65; Divine Power, 42, 44–5, 65, 132, 133; Divine Presence, 40, 48, 64, 93, 105, 114; Divine Remembrance, 77; Divine Speech, 78; Divine Unity, 75; Divine Wisdom, 116, 132; God's Light, 114; light of the knowledge of God, 135–7; link between knowledge of God/knowledge of the soul, 9; Manifestation of, 136, 137; Throne of the Essence, 15; see also Divine Actions; Divine Names; Divine Oneness

God as source of motivating thoughts (*khāṭir al-Ḥaqq*), xii–xiii, 1, 5, 7, 8, 17–18, 19, 22, 24, 27–8, 29; *khāṭir al-Ḥaqq/khāṭir al-Malak* distinction, 17; see also God; motivating thoughts, sources of

God-fearingness (*taqwā*), xiii, 7, 8, 12n, 26, 36–7; as the goal of knowledge, 135; God-fearingness and knowledge of God, 121–2, 135; key to the spiritual path, 122–3; knowledge of the soul, 9; purification of the soul by means of, 37; struggle against the ego, 13–14, 25

Ḥadīth: authentic *Ḥadīth*, 2, 6n, 10n, 13n, 26n, 29n, 60n, 93n; al-ʿAydarūs, ʿAbd al-Raḥmān b. Muṣṭafā, xii; 'Die before you die', 14; *The Fragrant Scent*, xiii; heart, expansion of, 59n; *jihād*, 13; on knowledge, 6, 9; prayer, 60; Qur'ān, 2; remembrance, 25–6; retreat, 94–7; Satan, 29, 134–5; spiritual guidance, 101; struggle against the ego, 13, 14; weak *Ḥadīth*, 93n, 135n

al-Ḥaḍramī, Aḥmad b. ʿUqba, 112

ḥāl, see spiritual state

ḥalāwa, see sweetness

al-Ḥallāj, al-Ḥusayn b. Mansūr, 12, 85–6

ḥaqā'iq, see verities

hawā, see base desire

heart (*qalb*), 3, 49; capitulation to the ego, 22–4; capitulation to the spirit, 23; darkness of, 7–8; death of, 108; directions from whence motivating thoughts arrive, 24; disclosure of God's light through the heart, 113–14; expansion of, 58–9, 64, 130; extinction and subsistence of, 51–2; heart/ego confusion, 23–4; knowledge of,

not being harmed by lack of, 38; remembrance during sleep, 85; unveiling during sleep, 81
solitude (*waḥda*), 92, 96, 97; see also retreat
soul (*nafs*): animal spirit, 34–5, 45; attributes of, 7; darkness of, 49, 76; dormant soul, 41; the highest discipline of the soul, 73; importance paid by the Prophet to the soul, 37–8; knowledge of, 9–10, 23, 101; link between knowledge of God/knowledge of the soul, 9; rational soul, 35, 36, 45, 62; reflection of the lights of the spirit on the heart and soul, 39–42; soul as locus for inspiration, 36; soul as locus for intellection, 36; stagnation of, 61; wishes of, 51–2; see also ego
spirit (*rūḥ*), 24; animal spirit, 34–5, 38, 45, 62; body/spirit connection, 68; difference between human and animal spirit, 36–7; Divine Essence, 49; free spirit, 46, 49; heart's capitulation to the spirit, 23; human spirit, 35, 45–6; as locus of love, 47; 'the Mother of the Book', 46; reflection of the lights of the spirit on the heart and soul, 39–42; Spirit of Sublime Command, 36, 37; spirituality, 40; Transcendent Spirit, 39; Universal Spirit, 50
spiritual audition (*samāʿ*), 90; People of Spiritual Audition, 90
spiritual descent, see *silsila*
spiritual discipline (*riyāḍa*), 41, 46
spiritual drunkenness, 12, 48
spiritual guidance, 54; finding spiritual guidance, 111–13; the form of the perfect office of spiritual guidance, 70–1; *Ḥadīth*, 101; the most perfect station in the office of spiritual guidance, 58–64; outstanding value of, 101–102; stages of, 74–5; see also spiritual guide
spiritual guide (*shaykh*), xiii; Absolute Spiritual Guide, 69–70; 'He who has no master has Satan as his imam', 70; languor, conduct in state of, 103–104; necessity of keeping the company of spiritual masters, 70, 71–3; perfected spiritual guide, 97–8, 103; retreat, 97–8, 99–100, 101–102; the spiritual wayfarer caught by divine attraction, 56–7, 58, 60–1, 65–6, 67–8, 69–70; the spiritually attracted caught by spiritual wayfaring, 58–60, 66, 69–70; see also spiritual guidance
spiritual insight (*wārid*), 18–19; definition, 18; spiritual insight/motivating thoughts distinction, 18–19
spiritual path (*ṭarīq*), 19–20, 122; keys to, xiii, 122–3
spiritual state (*ḥāl*), 3, 12, 54, 108, 109; definition, 111; elaboration of the states of the spiritual wayfarer, 65–9; release from the shackles of spiritual states, 65; spiritual states/stations relationship, 109–11; state of contentment, 109–11; state of extinction, 80; states of the gnostics, 83–6; works/spiritual states connection, 68–9
spiritual wayfarer (*sālik*), 53, 121; elaboration of the states of the spiritual wayfarer, 65–9; most feared things for, 113–15; spiritual wayfarers qualified for spiritual guidance, 55–7; see also spiritual wayfarer, categories of
spiritual wayfarer, categories of 53–5;

ʿ*ujb*, see conceitedness
ʿUmar b. al-Khaṭṭāb, 123–4
Umm Salama, 132
uns, see intimacy
unveiled (*jilwa*), 57, 58, 78
unveiling (*kashf*), 19, 65, 66, 69–70, 97–8, 107, 108; clear unveiling, 81–2; imaginal unveiling, 81; People of Unveiling, 48, 50, 83; spiritual unveiling, 81, 85; see also disclosure; unveiled; veil/veiling
uprightness (*istiqāma*), 25, 43n

veil/veiling, 19, 98, 105, 135–6, 137; body, a veil to the spirit, 46; disobedience, a veil for the heart, 122; ego, a veil between the servant and his Lord, 16, 66; heart (a luminous veil, 66; a veil between God and the servant, 113); *iḥtijāb*, 136; see also unveiling
verities (*ḥaqā'iq*), 19, 107; spiritual verities, 65, 68, 69; suprasensible verities, 80–1; verities of certitude, 124–5

waḥda, see solitude
wajd, see ecstasy
wārid, see spiritual insight
al-Wāsiṭī, Abū Bakr, 82
wird, see litany
witnessing (*mushāhada*), 47, 56, 58, 66, 78, 125
World (*ʿĀlam*): Higher World, 15, 64, 66, 76; Lower World, 15; Spiritual World, 39; this world, 14–15 (love of, 8, 9, 122); World of Causality, 42, 45, 65, 116; World of Command, 24, 34; World of Creation, 24, 34; World of Divine Oneness, 19; World of Divine Power, 42, 116; World of the Higher Intellects, 39; World of Inward Ultimate Reality, 65; World of the Spirits, 40, 46; World of the Transcendent Spirit, 39; World of the Unseen, 67, 80
worship: Angels, worship of, 66–7; base desire, 20; body, 66, 67; dissipation of the soul's stagnation, 61; motivating thoughts, 6; outward acts of, 100; prostration, 66, 67; 'showing off' during, 91, 106–107; sincere worship, 65, 66, 82; sweetness in acts of, 81–2; see also prayer; spiritual works

yaqīn, see certainty
Yūsuf b. Asbāṭ, 120

al-Zabīdī, Muḥammad Murtaḍā, x, xiin
ẓāhir, see outward aspect
Zarrūq, Aḥmad, 112n, 129
Zayd b. Aslam, 119
zuhd, see renunciation